Pursuing the
Good Life

PURSUING
THE
Good Life

REIGNITING YOUR PASSION FOR
LIVING A LIFE THAT MATTERS!

Mark J. Britzman, Ed.D.

PURSUING THE GOOD LIFE
REIGNITING YOUR PASSION FOR LIVING A LIFE THAT MATTERS!

iUniverse books may be ordered through booksellers or by contacting:

iUniverse
1663 Liberty Drive
Bloomington, IN 47403
www.iuniverse.com
1-800-Authors (1-800-288-4677)

ISBN: 978-1-4917-6284-4 (sc)
ISBN: 978-1-4917-6285-1 (e)
ISBN: 978-1-4917-6286-8 (hc)

Library of Congress Control Number: 2015903760

Print information available on the last page.

iUniverse rev. date: 05/21/2015

With *Pursuing the Good Life*, Mark has gifted us with his amazingly fun-to-read life journey and his easy-to-use, well-researched advice. Mark, just like you and me, is an individual who yearns to thrive in life and not settle for just getting through the week. Mark skillfully weaves his own true-life, often funny, sometimes self-deprecating stories with recent findings. It is a fun yet compelling book that inspires hope and offers realistic ways to make changes and perhaps transform your life forever.

—Dan Drenkow, MBA, director of information systems, Augustana College in Sioux Falls, South Dakota

I learned quickly that Dr. Mark Britzman possesses a deep knowledge about the goodness of life. His humble and positive nature helped me as an exchange student from Lebanon unleash my voice and talk about my family, country and culture that I love so much. Dr. Britzman is a living model of the beauty of humanity and was stunned with his unique ability to seek my passion within my soul and let it become nourished like a neglected seed that grows into a wonderful flower. He exudes respect for others and looks for opportunities to bring out the best in others with his wise and kind way of being. His precious words in this book are a gift to others including myself. With love and respect,

Maya Azzan, Baakline, Mont-Liban, Lebanon

Packed with truly valuable lessons that are thoughtful and reflective, this book truly reveals what it takes to live a life based on character. Mark is successful at piecing together stories that will tug at your emotions while stirring up insights that apply to the journey to strengthen character throughout one's life. Without a doubt, Mark writes the way he teaches—easy to understand but truly valuable and supportive in application. Like me, you will find insights, inspiration, and basic understanding of character on every page of this book.

—Dr. Gary Smit, internationally renowned trainer in character education and former superintendent

Dr. Mark Britzman is an inspiring human being and person of character. As a CHARACTER COUNTS!^{SM} National Trainer, he compassionately led educators to examine their thoughts and actions, while using personal life anecdotes to demonstrate how virtue was its own reward. Through his wise counsel, he's helped heal many relationships, and through Pursuing the Good Life, he's charted a clear road map to finding ultimate happiness. This book will enlighten anyone who truly values their relationships.

—Anthony Cube, Director, Alumni Marketing and Communications, UCLA Alumni Association

Mark has expertly identified how social dynamics work, how individuals react to each other, and how you take control of your own development. Life may appear easy, but it is not and it is often confusing. However, this book reminded me of the power of loving relationships and caring and respectful interactions as not only the right thing to do but also beneficial for others and self.

—Lex Dekkers, sales manager, Amsterdam area, Netherlands

In *Pursuing the Good Life*, Dr. Mark Britzman advocates that change is an inevitable part of everyone's life journey and that how one learns and grows from change determines one's quality of life. Developing a sense of purpose and meaning, compelling goals, interesting work, and meaningful relationships, as well as engaging in life and physical activity are all ways Mark challenges readers to pursue the good life. I found Dr. Britzman to be candid, funny, intelligent, personable, and caring in his writing, as well as having a knowledge of his field of education. I would highly recommend *Pursuing the Good Life*.

—Phil Baker, internationally acclaimed musician

Contents

Acknowledgments

- To my wife, Rhonda, whose smile, laughter, caring spirit, and amazing energy serve as an inspiring model of one who truly lives the good life;
- To my daughters, Kylee and Ali, who have enriched my life in so many ways;
- To my parents, Dar and Jo Britzman, who have given me all the love, stability, and encouragement needed to thrive in life;
- To my siblings, Shari Platek and Steve Britzman, who set the bar very high when it comes to working hard and accumulating so many meaningful accomplishments;
- To my friends, who accept me for who I am and occasionally laugh at my jokes;
- To my primary mentors, Dr. Robert E. Wubbolding, Dr. Howard B. Smith, and Dr. Frank Main, who believed in me enough to establish high expectations and helped refine my skills to better unleash my gifts and talents to effectively bring out the best in others; and
- To my past and current students who radiate a positive energy of hope and passion, and an ideal of making the world a better place,

Thank you for enriching my life and providing me an opportunity to make the world a slightly better place!

- A special thanks to Bailey Raml, my incredibly talented graduate student and likely future leader in the counseling profession, who suggested revisions for this book; and the teams at Caliber Creative and iUniverse, who engaged their amazing gifts and talents to make this book a reality.

Pursuing the Good Life: Counseling and Consulting, LLC

Part 1

Many of us are waiting for happiness.

—Sonya Lyumbomirsky

One evening when my daughter Kylee, who was only a toddler at the time, came out from her bedroom and stated, "Daddy, I can't get to sleep," I responded, "What's wrong, sweetie?" She replied, "I can't get to sleep, because my teeth are wet." After a brief moment of irritation, I could not help but smile. I stated that she could stay up a moment or two and dry her teeth off and then go back to bed. My anticipated annoyance quickly disappeared. I marveled at her eagerness to creatively extend her day. My younger daughter, Ali, also displayed her joy for life when she was a toddler by getting so excited with anticipation that she would wave her arms up and down. Her pure joy reminded me of the potential to be consumed with delight and thrive in feelings of sheer delight.

What will be your response when you go to bed tonight? Will you have an intense feeling of disappointment that the day is about to end? Do you still have times when you struggle to sleep because you're too excited about squeezing a few more minutes out of the day? Can you develop sustained contentment as e-mails are likely pouring into your inbox and voice mail messages accumulate regardless of the day or time? My response too often at the end of the day has been, "Yes! I survived the day without any major problems!"

I want to preserve my integrity and begin with the following disclaimer: I do not have any magical quick fix to simulate that playful innocence of childhood. Is it even possible to recreate similar feelings of enthusiasm as we age and contain our emotions? I realize it is hard to have a peaceful feeling as your to-do list accrues. I, too, struggle at times with feelings of worry, anxiety, and dread related to the endless amount of things that need to be attended to.

Defining happiness can be as elusive as achieving it. Many in the field of psychology scoff at the concept and so prefer to claim happiness is a subjective feeling of well-being. However, many experts in psychology and counseling agree that happiness is the by-product of pursuing a good life, freedom from chronic stress and suffering, flourishing, well-being, joy, prosperity, and pleasure (Anchor 2013; Hanson 2013).

Pursuing the good life has been a quest for philosophers throughout recent human history as life became more than just surviving the many dangers of the day. A central question that perhaps has become even more important is, What makes life worth living? Industrial and technological advances have been pervasive and have provided significantly longer life spans concurrently with new discoveries. The resulting new evolutionary and scientific discoveries have provided greater insight and deeper questions related to our overall purpose in a universe that appears to be expanding toward a sense of infinity.

The indescribable fast pace of new knowledge today has provided further insight into the pursuit of happiness, which was quite a novel goal stated by Thomas Jefferson when drafting the Declaration of Independence; there is still debate regarding his primary influence. Many attribute the goal to John Locke, an English philosopher and physician regarded as one of the most influential of Enlightenment thinkers. In his seminal book *Essay Concerning Human Understanding*, he stated, "The highest perfection of intellectual nature lies in a careful and constant pursuit of true and solid happiness" (Locke, 1689, Section 51).

I am delighted you have taken the time from your busy schedule to read this book and reflect on whether the psychological good life is worthy of pursuit, or even possible in today's era of time poverty. The fields of counseling and psychology have essentially evolved as very humanistic and strength-based models for promoting psychological well-being in a variety of contexts. Positive psychology, often described as the scientific study of what makes life worth living, added a renewed quest for valid research and developed meta-analysis of studies that provided data and insight regarding primary impacts on happiness. "What is good in life is not simply the absence of what is problematic" (Peterson 2013, 4).

Kylee—just loving life …

It is perfectly normal for you to ask, "My life is all right, but is this as good as it gets?" "Why don't I feel happier?" This mind-set is often followed by blaming yourself for not being more positive. "I could be living in a third-world country with famine and disease. What is wrong with me?" You then begin to worry and borrow imagined problems from the future. If you feel this way, you are not alone. Most people obviously want to be happier and help others actualize their potential but perhaps get lost in a very busy world. This book was written for you and will provide you an opportunity to self-evaluate and seize opportunities to make choices that are more life-enriching. Welcome to a better present and future!

Many of us struggle with an onslaught of items added to our to-do list. "I should check my e-mail, return some of my voice mail messages, get some groceries, do some cleaning, prepare for the upcoming week, make sure the car is maintained, and so on." Minor tasks flow into your life, and sometimes significant distress can also arrive without notice. There appears no reprieve unless you can take a nap; and if you do, you may suffer from a tinge of guilt. Life becomes a treadmill that no longer seems to stop, and the goal is just to survive the week.

Pursuing the good life entails clarifying your hopes and dreams, finding an optimal direction that moves you closer to what you want, self-evaluating the consequences of your choices, and consistently developing a plan that is need-fulfilling. Drawing from the fields of counseling, positive psychology, social psychology, and clinical psychology has reinforced ingredients that facilitate positive feelings and heightened well-being. Peterson (2013) describes major factors that contribute to psychological health and pursuing a good life, included but not limited to the following:

- experiencing more positive feelings than negative feelings;
- being satisfied with life;
- identifying and using talents and strengths;
- being engaged in activities;

- having close relationships with neighbors, colleagues, friends, and family members;
- being a contributing member of a social community; and
- having meaning and purpose (p. 19).

Every choice you make has a consequence. Your total behavior consists of thinking, doing, feeling, and physiology. You have the most control over your thinking and doing that impact how you feel and your overall health and wellness. However, all are interdependent (Glasser 2011; Wubbolding 2010). This book will allow you an opportunity to heighten your awareness of ingredients that promote fullness of life. You can then develop greater clarity about what makes you feel better about your life. The benefits of feeling happier are connected to knowing the good, loving the good, and doing the good. Pursuing the good life requires developing a greater purpose and meaning in life, seizing opportunities to enrich relationships, making need-fulfilling and healthy choices, and strengthening your character and resilience by doing the right thing even when it costs you more than you want to pay at times. Your journey can be fueled by additional healthy choices related to your wellness, which not only help you develop greater resilience and ability to handle adversity and distress, but also facilitate additional positive energy to thrive in life rather than just survive the day.

However, if making the necessary choices that increase happiness were easy, everyone would be pursuing a life that leads to sustained joy rather than short-term pleasure. Temporary mood enhancers are available to many on a daily basis and too often relate to overindulgent choices related to alcohol abuse, drug dependence, overspending, binging on high sugar and fat foods, and so on. Short-term emotional highs only serve as fool's gold, with no sustaining value, and too often provide a temporary haven for feeling better. The inevitable emotional crash often creates a greater need to frantically look for a quick fix to feel better. Psychologists, of course, have a fancy word phrase to describe this process, called the hedonistic treadmill. Sadly, many people just try to get through each day by seeking temporary joy or diversions. Ultimately, unhealthy choices lead to a host of mental health disorders, including but not limited to anxiety and depression. Negative emotions can call out what is not working for you and provide opportunities to make better choices, perhaps even a new path in life. We all have made poor choices, and lessons can be learned from the bad times in life that may even toughen us up and allow us to develop a greater capacity of delight when we have the opportunity to make life better.

I, too, am a work in progress. My mind can easily wander to the negative. I then often denigrate myself for not being more positive with self-statements: "Why is it so difficult to remind myself about my wonderful family, deep friendships, talented colleagues, inspiring mentors, and passionate students?" I, too, want to be more positive, and perhaps that is the purpose of an insatiable thirst for learning new and well-researched strategies to pursue the good life. Perhaps a person who has it all together would not have the same passion I do for this topic. However, not having it all together and still wanting to pursue the good life is the quest for most of us. Writing this book for you is ironically very helpful for me to be reminded of the ingredients necessary to not only survive a long day but also thrive in a life that often feels too short.

I also realize that some self-help books can ironically promote you to feel worse about your situation. Misguided advice that a good life consists of being rich and successful is an illusion. Well, that might be true if you wrote the book selling information that has massive appeal, but it is the psychological equivalent of purchasing snake oil to cure serious ailments. Many self-help gurus have big egos and narcissistic tendencies; they create an illusion of instant gratification with promises of success that is often associated with having more of something that often relates to money and materialism. To keep the treadmill going, you have to replenish the juice of joy by making more money and buying more stuff. You then habituate to what you have and create a perpetual cycle of wanting more and more. You might be thinking to yourself, *Wow, this author is just jealous and must unconsciously want his own afternoon television show.* Truthfully,

I want to be helpful for you and retain an inner peace by promoting the good life without prostituting my integrity. I honestly want to be helpful and retain a sense of satisfaction that this book is deemed helpful for you. I can then go bed tonight feeling a sense of inner peace, as I believe it is true that, "The best pillow is a clear conscience."

Consequently, this book contains much more than psychological sound bites. To reap the benefits, it will necessitate you exploring a new path by developing a plan that fulfills the need for love and belonging, empowerment, fun and enjoyment, and freedom and independence, and achieves higher states of good health and wellness. This is the impetus for me writing a book that will help you pursue a good life via practical strategies that emanate from valid research in the fields of professional counseling and psychology. I hope you appreciate a few personal anecdotes, some perhaps funny and others maybe not so much. However, illuminating my blunders and behavioral sinkholes provides a sense of humility, humanness, and teachable moments.

Certified as a Glasser Scholar and Trainer with the help of my mentor Dr. Robert Wubbolding in Scotland and Ireland

Chapter 1

Developing a Capacity for Delight

The capacity for delight is the gift of paying attention.
—Julia Margaret Cameron

Do you believe happiness is a choice? How much of good feelings are generated by external events and environments, and what internally helps you discover greater joy and fulfillment? Researchers have recently defined happiness as the radiation of joy over one's entire existence or a deep sense of flourishing that arises from making healthy choices. Shawn Anchor, author of *The Happiness Advantage* and a former instructor at Harvard, studies the science of happiness. He claims you can change your health, relationships, work, energy, and life in general. He believes happiness is the fuel that actually impacts every aspect of your life. Students do better on tests when their brains are positive. You are more successful at work when you determine an optimal mind-set. Happiness improves and nourishes your brain functioning.

Many self-experts claim this, but there is a hollowness without research. For instance, longitudinal studies were done of nuns who wrote down their perceptions of their lives in the 1930s. Nuns, by the way, are a good experimental group because their days are somewhat uniform regarding dress, nutrition, and daily rituals. Their logs were then objectively analyzed by a team of researchers and categorized into areas of happiness based on their journal entries. Interestingly, 54 percent of the so-called happy nuns lived to age ninety-four, while only 15 percent of the unhappy nuns lived to age ninety-four. Living a long and unhappy life is not compelling, but the replication of these studies appears to produce valid and similar results (Anchor 2013).

The beauty of a loving relationship—a mom and her daughters!

What is your vision of a good life?

What are you doing when you experience feelings of sustained happiness? There is a high likelihood that you are most content with your life when you are making choices that satisfy certain basic needs. However, do you know what these needs are; and if so, do you have a vision and plan to make consistent choices to ensure feeling good about your life?

There appear to be basic human needs that are universal. There is a high likelihood that these needs are genetically programmed and are with us from birth until death. These needs when satisfied can lead to feelings of happiness and joy. Conversely, painful feelings are common when the needs are not met consistently.

Human beings are incredibly resilient, and our physiology is programmed for us to live a long life, depending on our genetic makeup and choices to promote or deter our overall sense of wellness. Furthermore, the need is not only to survive but to thrive. We also seem to have a need for love and belonging. It is likely that some of your most satisfying experiences entail interacting with those whom you respect and admire. In contrast, some of your most painful memories probably are associated with times when you were criticized, blamed, or put down by others. In an optimal environment, we seem to naturally want to make choices that enhance our sense of significance and feelings of self-worth. It feels good to be recognized and admired for who we are as well as our accomplishments.

We also seem to have a need for freedom to be in control of our lives and make choices without coercion, threats, or bribery from others or the external world. It simply feels good to be in charge of our destiny. There is a high likelihood that you have produced quality results when you were allowed to be in charge of an assignment or project. Freedom is intimately linked to internal motivation.

Lastly, we have a need for fun and enjoyment. Life appears to be more demanding as one goes through childhood and adolescence and enters adulthood. The careless joy, laughter, and permission to allow ourselves to enjoy the moment are often trumped by increasing life demands, responsibilities, and a tendency to worry and ruminate about the future. Consequently, the need for fun goes unfulfilled unless you choose time for activities, hobbies, and leisure pursuits that you enjoy. It is sad that too many of us do not seize opportunities for enjoyable activities for a variety of reasons, including but not limited to lack of time or perhaps feeling guilty that we should be doing something else on our endless to-do lists (Glasser 2011; Wubbolding 2010).

Perhaps meeting basic needs seems very self-serving, superficial, and even hedonistic. If you believe I left out something very important, you are both right and wrong. You are right in the sense that I did not specifically mention the need for spirituality and faith. Ironically, the search for love, the desire for significance, and the yearning for freedom from external control are important in your quest to deepen your purpose and meaning as you pursue the good life.

You can certainly change your circumstances, especially if you are in a very unsatisfying location, relationship, or job. However, external factors contribute only a small percentage; many researchers believe approximately 10 percent of your overall sense of well-being is linked to external factors unless you are living in poverty, ravaged by addictions, or in a disrespectful significant relationship. You also have a genetic tendency that relates to your temperament and disposition, but you can change your brain. Even for identical twins, which on average are remarkably similar, further depth in research findings indicate that there are identical twins with significant differences in the way they experience their world and life (Anchor 2013).

Thriving in life and resulting feelings of happiness and well-being is a choice that facilitates movement toward pursuing the good life. Peterson (2013) stated that recent research reveals the following:

- Most people are generally happy.
- Happiness often begets more satisfaction, as it leads to desirable outcomes in school, work, fulfilling social relationships, and even good health and a longer life span on average.
- Most people are resilient and bounce back from adversity.
- Happiness strengthens character, which leads to positive relationships and helps serve as a buffer against the discouraging impact of disappointments and setbacks.

- The strength of one's character is often revealed during times of crisis.
- Other people matter and relationships are primary influencers of a meaningful life.
- Spirituality and religion matter.
- Satisfying work can provide greater meaning and purpose.
- Money makes an ever-diminishing contribution to well-being, unless it is used in a charitable way to help others.
- The "heart" matters more than the "head," and educators must focus not only on critical thinking but need to be teaching unconditional caring and kindness.
- Good days typically entail a sense of autonomy, competence, accomplishment, and positive connection with others.
- The good life can be taught!

Self-evaluation becomes a skill that allows you to understand the consequences of your choices and overall direction in life.

- Physical activity initiates a cascade of successes throughout the day.
- Develop the capacity of delight via meditation, prayer, relaxation, or just deep breathing and focus on the present or what is right in your life, thus developing a greater capacity for delight.
- Enriched relationships are the primary key related to fullness in life.
- Find a field of study or work that matters to you.

(Anchor 2013; Ben-Shahar 2007; Fredrickson 2009; Glasser 2011; Meyers 2000; Peterson 2013; Rath 2007; Ricard 2011; Wubbolding 2010).

Pursuing the good life can begin by taking an inventory of what is going well in your life presently. Counting your blessings and not your afflictions has both pragmatic value and research support (Wubbolding

2010). To pursue the good life necessitates taking an inventory of life, slowing down, and noticing what is right or even beautiful in your life now. I spent too much time in the past ruminating on what I could have done better and worrying about worst-case scenarios in the future. Ironically, all I really have is this present moment.

What provides you with feelings of happiness and delight?

How do you know what choices are linked to short-term pleasure or long-term sustained joy? Seemingly too many people look for temporary highs, such as alcohol, drugs, sex without love, and so on because it gives them a temporary rush of pleasure. When asked why they engage in this self-destructive behavior, they'll likely tell you it is fun and they want to have a good time that makes them feel good. The intense pleasure will likely evaporate, leaving a sense of emptiness and perhaps shame that sets the stage for searching for a more powerful mood alterer.

Although life is often challenging and bad things can happen to good people like you as we have so many responsibilities as adults, it is possible to react to adversity in a hopeful and resilient manner with effort, grit, and determination. Your journey is also facilitated by enjoying present moments, strengthening character, enriching relationships, and making healthy and need-fulfilling choices each day. You can then reap the consequences of greater meaning, purpose, and sustained joy.

Try to imagine what would make you happier.

- A 70″ improved high-definition television that is curved?
- A new car?
- Living in a warm climate?
- Winning the lottery?
- Retirement?

Perhaps a few readers remember what life was like in the 1940s. Approximately one-third of homes did not have running water, indoor toilets, or a bathtub or shower, and more than half had no central heating. Sixty percent of adults over twenty-five years of age had an eighth-grade education, with only 25 percent earning a high school degree and only 5 percent graduating from college.

Now, compare that with living in today's world, where the typical household has running water, at least two bathrooms, and central heating, and is typically equipped with microwave ovens, dishwashers, flat-screen televisions, personal computers, and of course iPads and cell phones.

When asked to rate their level of happiness, individuals living in the 1940s reported being "very happy," with an average score of 7.5 on a ten-point scale. The average score today is 7.2. Hmmm … why don't all these extra gadgets and luxuries make us significantly happier (Haidt, 2006)?

What generally tends to make you happier?

Sonja Lyumbomirsky (2007), an internationally renowned social psychologist and author of *The How of Happiness: A Scientific Approach to Getting the Life You Want*, states that happiness often refers to the experience of joy, contentment, or positive well-being, combined with a sense that one's life is good, meaningful, and worthwhile (p. 52).

Positive psychologists originally concluded that we have a genetic set point for happiness that accounts for approximately 50 percent of how we generally feel. Our circumstances (e.g., income, home, climate we live in, etc.) appear to only account for about 10 percent of our total happiness. Fortunately, however, that leaves an additional 40 percent of happiness that is totally within our control via attitudes and choices. However, now it is widely accepted that happiness is dynamic, and we not make broad and general statements regarding concrete percentages. The causes of well-being can better be understood as a pie chart of influencers rather than fixed percentages (Peterson 2013).

There are many myths when it comes to determining the optimal pathway to experience a happier state. Many of us believe if I only had (you fill in the blank), I would be happier. Or, if I could just change my circumstances (e.g., job, home, car, etc.), I would be happier. And lastly, many of us belief that happiness is something you either have or don't have.

The truth is that we tend to adapt to our circumstances, both good and bad, fairly quickly. It is true that you will likely be happier if you are blessed with good genes and optimal circumstances. Fortunately, however, we do have some control over our feelings of happiness that can be attributed to the attitudes and behaviors we choose each and every day.

The good news is there are so many ways that I have researched and experienced that make life more meaningful, and yes—happier! There are even times when I feel great and can't wait for the next day. I am putting forth effort to try to make those days more the norm rather than the exception. I would like you to join me on a journey toward being more appreciative and grateful for the goodness in life, as well as preparing ourselves for the inevitable adversity and challenges that lurk ahead.

There is actually a science of happiness that relates to recent findings in the human brain. You can literally train your brain to become happier. A more "positive brain" is linked to every domain of your life. As Richard Hanson, PhD, stated in his seminal book entitled *Hardwiring Happiness* (2013),

> All mental activity – sights and sounds, thoughts and feelings, conscious and unconscious processes – is based on underlying neural activity. Much mental and therefore neural activity flows through the brain like ripples on a river, with no lasting effects on its channel. But intense, prolonged, or repeated

mental/neural activity – especially if it is conscious – will leave
an enduring imprint in neural structure, like a surging current
reshaping a riverbed. As they say in neuroscience: Neurons
that fire together wire together. Mental states become neural
traits. Day after day, your mind is building your brain. (p. 10).

However, you can develop a positive mind-set by trying to savor
the good times longer with additional focused attention to become
more aware of your mental processes without choosing via autopilot
habitual choices and ingrained habits (Peterson 2013; Siegel 2011).
For instance, what do you think about when taking a shower? Having
warm water and feeling clean can be a positive contributor to your
overall sense of well-being, but only if you intentionally try to be
mindful and enjoy the experience. Taking a shower and ruminating
about your seemingly endless to-do list is probably not as satisfying.
Being more aware of the present with greater clarity helps explore
our inner lives, which promotes more intentional and need-fulfilling
choices and resulting activities based on what is needed at any given
moment. This keen awareness can significantly improve almost every
aspect of your life, especially if you can focus on the now of your
experience. Savoring contributes to your well-being and necessitates
sharing positive experiences with others, immersing yourself in an
activity, and diverting yourself when you try to dampen a pleasant
experience with unwanted self-statements and thoughts.

To illustrate the power of the mind, Dr. Jonathan Haidt, who
is a professor at the University of Virginia, asked 350 students in his
introductory psychology class to engage in four activities. One of the
activities was to indulge the senses, as by taking a break for ice cream
in the middle of the afternoon and then savoring the ice cream. This
activity was really enjoyable, but like all pleasures, it faded quickly.
The other three activities were potentially gratifications: attend a
lecture or class that you don't normally go to, perform an act of
kindness for a friend who could use some cheering up, and write
down the reasons you are grateful to someone and later call or visit

that person to express your gratitude. Dr. Haidt's most significant findings were that people experienced longer-lasting improvements in mood from kindness and gratitude activities than from those in which they indulged themselves. In fact, many students stated their good feelings continued on into the next day—which no one said about eating the ice cream (Haidt 2006).

Seeking pleasure is very tempting; satisfaction sometimes can be obtained via healthy behaviors such as a back rub or enjoying a warm breeze. However, gratifications often come from using one's strengths to accomplish something, learn something, or improve something. They are much more enduring and often jump-start other meaningful and altruistic endeavors.

What choices appear to impact your level of an overall sense of well-being? Ironically, there is little relationship between money and materialistic items and sustained positive feelings. In fact, as Dr. David Meyers articulates in his book *The Pursuit of Happiness*, "Money is two steps removed from happiness: Actual income doesn't much influence happiness; how satisfied we are with our income does. If we are content with how much it is, we're likely to say we're happy" (1992, 39). Recent research presents mixed results regarding the relationship between money and happiness. However, wealthy people apparently take less pleasure in the small things in life, perhaps because they already have big things. Why don't all these extra gadgets and comforts make us significantly happier? Perhaps it's because our behaviors and thoughts directly impact our feelings and physiology (Anchor 2013).

It is likely that some of our most satisfying experiences entail interacting with those whom we respect and admire. In an optimal environment, we seem to want to make choices that enhance our sense of significance and feelings of self-worth. We also seem to have a need for freedom to be in control of our lives and to make choices without coercion, threats, or bribery from others or the external world. We have a need for fun and enjoyment. Throughout life, we have a need to experience enjoyable leisure pursuits.

Seemingly, happiness is a profound choice that is sustained by satisfying needs in a healthy and consistent fashion, often regardless of external circumstances (Ricard 2003). Victor Frankl, an Austrian psychiatrist as well as a Holocaust survivor, stated: "What man actually needs is not a tensionless state, but rather the striving and struggling for some goal worthy of him. What he needs is not the discharge of tension at any cost, but the call of a potential meaning waiting to be fulfilled by him" (Ben-Shahar 2007).

The number one condition that trumps all others when it comes to predicting happiness, according to a myriad of research studies, is enriched relationships. Conversely, annoying and conflictual relationships are one of the surest ways to reduce your happiness. The best ingredients for enriched relationships are the demonstration of good character, which includes integrity, honesty, respect, and altruism. That is why character will always matter as you pursue a fulfilling and happy life (Anchor 2013).

Gratitude is an effective way to experience sustained happiness and well-being. Seemingly, happiness is reinforced by using your gifts to seize opportunities to bring out the best in others and thus make our world a better place. What activities give you leads to sustained joy, contentment, and greater purpose in life?

When are you most likely to feel a sense of inner peace?

The new wave in psychology that appears to cultivate an inner peace is the practice of mindfulness. This entails finding a mental state where you are able to engage, let go of unhealthy thoughts, and accept whatever emotions you encounter. You can invite even negative emotions into the present and learn to let them go, just like a leaf falling into a stream. You can concurrently expand your awareness and open up your senses to engage in the present. Furthermore, you can really clarify and live in harmony with values that are most important to you, for example, love, peace, hope, respect, and compassion. Richard Hanson (2013) stated, "Staying mindful entails staying with the present moment by moment. Mindfulness itself only witnesses, but alongside that witnessing could be active, goal-directed efforts to nudge your mind one way or another" (p. 8).

How often throughout the day do you notice what you are experiencing in the present? What are you seeing, hearing, and smelling, and how are you feeling? Horace Mann once stated, "Yesterday, somewhere between sunrise and sunset, two golden hours, each set with sixty diamond minutes. No reward is offered, for they are gone forever." This quote serves as a reminder about the consequences of not becoming still and noticing the beauty of the outdoors, a smile on someone's face, a warm shower, or the taste of a wonderful meal. We want to be goal-directed, but not governed. That is, we often borrow problems from the future when we lust for things and worry about what might happen. Peterson (2013) reviewed data from a large survey regarding how most people spent their day. The most frequent activities included, "sleeping; working; doing household chores; eating and drinking; caring for others; engaging in leisure pursuits or sports, and providing service through formal organizations" (p. 11). The miscellaneous or other category revealed an inordinate time was also spent shopping, talking on the phone, grooming, caring for pets, and dealing with e-mail. Our biggest nemesis is often impatience. What is the point of saving time if we don't use it to savor what makes life compelling?

The lack of time can set the foundation for something that will make us feel better right now! Material items can be purchased easily, as we are bombarded with advertisements that can trigger emotional desires. Many of these items are perhaps perceived as being better than what we currently own. For instance, new cellular phones, computers, tablets, vehicles, and homes have improved features. We constantly seem to have to rejuice the juice of joy. Can you imagine having a black-and-white television with three channels and no remote control?

We are blessed, however, to have numerous parents who tirelessly try to give their children what they need to thrive in life. On a daily basis, numerous educators, school counselors, and administrators are dedicating their entire professional careers to help students develop competence and good character, which build a foundation for lifelong learning and productive citizenship. Furthermore, we have numerous leaders whose lives are filled with integrity and moral courage. Yes, there are so many people in our community who really try to and do make our world a better place and serve as an inspiration.

As Stephen Covey articulates so well in his 2006 book entitled *Everyday Greatness*, "The majority of people in this world are good people doing good things, and that we should not let the noise of the negative minority drown out the steady sound of good that is around us" (p. viii).

We all applaud the many isolated heroic acts of courage, but the goodness that lives on really comes from ordinary people doing extraordinary things even when there is a cost.

Every day we have an opportunity to make choices that promote helping us become trustworthy, respectful, responsible, fair, caring, and good citizens. Please be reminded that character will never go away as long as individuals are thinking, acting, and feeling. We can choose to be more intentional about teaching, advocating, and modeling good character or give in to a life full of cynicism that entails "I can't really much make a difference, and kids will be kids."

Stephen Covey challenges us all with three important questions:

"Is your life like driftwood being tossed to and fro, or are you instead making your own waves and going in directions you - by choice - want to go?

"To what ends, or purposes, are your daily choices leading? To what ends, or purposes, would you like them to lead?"

"Is your life in harmony with timeless, universal principals?" (Covey 2006, xv).

These questions are answered by the choices we make on a daily basis.

Someone once asked me, "When will your train arrive at the station?" This question, couched in metaphor, was a reminder of being on the treadmill that actually may never lead to fulfillment because the journey of life is not enjoyed. For instance, "I will only be happy when I _____" Is feeling more confident an act of assurance or a trust that an action will get you to a better place?

> If you keep resting your mind on self-criticism, worries, grumbling about others, hurts, and stress, then your brain will be shaped into greater reactivity, vulnerability to anxiety and depressed mood, a narrow focus on threats and losses, and inclinations toward anger, sadness, and guilt. (Hanson, 2013, 11).

You will likely never feel fully confident, and fear is a part of life. The paradox is that triumph through fear breeds confidence, combined with rejoicing with your current successes and how far you have come in your life's journey. It is true that the psychologically rich tend to become richer!

Integration Opportunity

What is your vision of a good life?

What provides you with feelings of happiness and delight?

What generally tends to make you happier?

When are you most likely to feel a sense of inner peace?

Chapter 2

Welcoming Eustress

**I promise you nothing is as chaotic as it seems.
Nothing is worth your health. Nothing is worth
poisoning yourself into stress, anxiety, and fear.**

—Steve Maraboli

How much do you stretch your comfort zone? Are there times when you would give anything not to have any stress in your life? I hope not because without stress, you have a condition called rigor followed by its cousin mortis, and yes—you would be dead. Your body has been beautifully created to need an optimal level of stress to not only function, but to make choices that impact your health and wellness. Life is often challenging, and situational adversity is inevitable. We cannot control many hardships; however, we are able to build a resilience and not allow distress to exceed our capacity to cope.

However, there are millions of individuals that continue to struggle with overwhelming feelings of anxiety. The symptoms tend to manifest in the following ways. Panic disorders include increased arousal, hyperventilation, dizziness, and often nausea. Generalized anxiety is a sense of worry or dread that lasts at least six months and robs one of pleasure. Social phobias are usually associated with individuals that avoid settings and activities that cause them to blush, shake, or even sweat. Anxiety disorders can lead to exhaustion and often swirls with a mixture of depression. Small irritations can often feel like very serious problems (Wehrenberg 2008).

Anxiety often has multiple causes linked to a genetic propensity for being hypersensitive, overexaggerating the seriousness of real-life events, and then avoiding what may scare you the most. Avoidance ironically brings about more distress, worry, and rumination. The good news is that even though feeling anxious is not pleasant, it can be modified to an optimal level that makes you feel more passionate and energetic. To accomplish this, you must learn to literally have more control of your brain chemistry (Anchor 2013).

Your brain consists of soft nervous tissue contained in the skull of vertebrates, functioning as the coordinating center of sensation and intellectual and nervous activity. It has many incredible functions, including a complicated maze of ten billion neurons, each of which connects with ten thousand other neurons. Wow, your cells and the complex network are almost infinite. Recent research with incredible technology has helped to better understand the brain's ability to change throughout your lifetime. That ability is often referred to as plasticity, and it really means neurons that fire together wire together.

The complex interconnection of neurotransmitters such as dopamine, serotonin, glutamate, gamma aniobutyric acid (i.e., GABA), and norepinephrine has the most impact on feelings of anxiety. Your sympathetic nervous system can produce too much anxiety when your hypothalamus sends messages to your adrenal glands to release adrenaline and cortisol, which are needed to release stores of energizing fuel such as glucose and fat that helps your muscles work hard. Bursts of energy can be helpful—but only when you need to act quickly to outwit something dangerous. Your stress response cannot be called into action constantly for a prolonged period of time without some sense of relief and rest. An optimal balance of neurochemical reactions is necessary as your brain is monitoring much of your functioning and impacts your overall mood.

Each neurochemical has its specific role but affects your nervous system, stress response, limbic system, basal ganglia, and cortex. This is an oversimplification, but when there are minor imbalances in neurotransmitters, you can literally experience symptoms. Your hippocampus, which is part of the limbic, registers details from your experience and sends them to your primary areas of executive functioning, found in the cortex. The amygdala registers all emotions and almost serves like a smoke detector that goes off when it recognizes your need to survive a situation that is either real or just perceived as threatening. Appropriate explanations of the brain would necessitate an entire book, but the primary goal in decreasing overwhelming feelings of anxiety is to have more control over the parasympathetic nervous system so that you can calm yourself down, breathe properly, relax, and find proper perspective so your amygdala and hippocampus work together to differentiate what is really dangerous from what is not. There are techniques that can quiet the part of your brain that tends to develop the fight-or-flight response (Wehrenberg 2008).

Ironically, real and perceived stress is not something you want to fight or flee. Research indicates that even at high levels, stress can often create greater mental toughness, deeper relationships, heightened awareness, new perspectives, a sense of mastery, and greater appreciation of life and the blessings you do have. These benefits, however, necessitate a positive mind-set and require that you look at the situation from a different perspective. It may be comforting to you that our brains have actually evolved with a built-in negativity bias.

"While the bias emerged in harsh settings very different from our own, it continues to operate inside us today as we drive in traffic, head into a meeting, settle a sibling squabble, tri to diet, watch the news, juggle household, pay bills, or go on a date. Your brain has a hair-trigger readiness to go negative to help you survive" (Hanson 2013, 20).

The antidote to the physical feeling of being afraid is to be very careful that you do not intake too many stress-enhancing substances such as caffeine, alcohol, tobacco, sugar, and even excessive sweeteners, which all have the potential to trigger feelings of panic. Minimizing demands related to communication can help as well. That is, try to compartmentalize responding to phone calls, e-mails, and text messages instead of letting them alert your brain throughout the day. Taking breaks and finding low-stimulation environments, such as going for a short walk, can also have many benefits, allowing you to get away from the noise of stressful environments. Even taking a look outside or at a favorite picture, or walking down a hallway, can produce some symptom relief. Your mind, body, and soul, like everything else in life, need time to recover. Prayer, meditation, yoga, listening to music, journaling, creative drawing, and frequently spending time outside are helpful, especially when combined with deep breathing and a focus on your senses. This automatically calms the mind down and makes rumination and worry more challenging. Nutritious food and physical activity will further provide the positive energy and resilience to handle the rigors of each and every day (Anchor 2013; Wehrenberg 2008).

What are your biggest fears in life?

This sounds easy, but I realize it is very challenging at times. A primary fear of most every parent is that something tragic will happen to your child. I remember a time in my life when I was under a great deal of distress. Nearly everything felt out of my control. My infant daughter had been in the hospital for numerous days with the RSV virus and was not getting better. Furthermore— and far less important—the counseling agency that I directed was having its accreditation visit. I was also supposed to be in charge of a fundraising project. Loved ones suggested I take a quick break and go work out at the gym. Instead, I tried to go back to work to get a few things done so I could go back to the hospital and be with my daughter. I was driving, and my car died at the busiest intersection. The situation was exacerbated by the beginning of a snowstorm on a brutally cold January day. Other drivers appeared irritated as I slowed the normal traffic flow during noon lunch hour.

I was about to give up on anyone stopping to help me until a homeless person who was riding a bike (yes, with temperatures below freezing and snow beginning to blanket the road) stopped and asked me if he could help by pushing my car to across the intersection. Interestingly, others helped as well, and I was able to park out of traffic (although I received a ticket later since it was not close enough to the curb). I called my wife, Rhonda, who has an excellent ability to provide useful advice when I am confused and stressed, and asked her what I should do. She stated, "Don't worry; we will get through this." Those are hard words to hear if you are a psychologist. She stated, "Just call the car dealer and have your car repaired."

I went back to the hospital after the car was towed so I could be with my daughter. I could feel the by-products of stress, fueled by ruminating thoughts of worst-case scenarios. Thankfully we were told that Ali was finally recovering after a long week in the hospital. I then called the car dealer service shop and inquired about the status of my vehicle, which I had already prediagnosed with transmission failure. I don't know anything about cars, but I had that problem previously, and it was the only language I used when I believed there was a serious problem with my vehicle. The serviceman, who knew me by name, said, "Mark, I know you are stressed out and I am not sure how to tell you this, but it should be good news." I remember thinking *How can it be good news? Transmission repair is expensive. We will also have significant medical bills.* He stated, "Well, we found the problem." I braced myself, and he informed me, "You ran out of gas." My immediate response was that obviously the gas gauge did not work. However, he assured me it did, and his last words were, "We filled your car with gas, and you are ready to go."

Ali, feeling so much better!

Integration Opportunity

How do you know when your distress exceeds your capacity to cope?

How many of the things you worried about last year actually came true?

What helps you become aware of irrational thoughts?

How do you effectively dispute and change maladaptive self-statements and faulty beliefs?

What helps you soften your strong emotional reactions?

What helps you focus on your present senses (e.g., sights, sounds, feelings, smells, etc.)?

What gives you a sense of inner peace that everything will probably be just fine?

Part 2

Knowing what makes us pursue the good life is not enough to experience it. We must be motivated to become engaged in using our strengths and talents and also seize opportunities to bring out the best in each other. This process necessitates a plan and an optimal direction. Self-awareness combined with internal motivation is a powerful fuel that propels us along the path of sustained joy and happiness.

Seeing the negatives in life is seemingly a common human foible. Psychology for too long seemed half-baked. There has historically been a myopic focus on human weaknesses, mental disorders, and psychopathology. I look forward to a future where there are more books about human strengths, virtues, and inspiring stories of compassionate deeds. Sadly, bad news still sells, and the manuals that categorize mental health disorders seem to get thicker with each new edition. Why is there such a fascination with abnormal behavior?

Reality is skewed and resides in our perceptions of events and happenings in the world. There are actually many individuals that lead fulfilling and meaningful lives and even feel happy despite challenges. Why is it not more compelling to study the ingredients of those that not only pursue a good life but experience one on a daily basis?

The good news is that there is a growing movement that is researching and finding universal truths that facilitate happiness, sustained joy, and inner peace. The following chapters distill complicated research into pragmatic opportunities that discover the optimal paths that lead to a rich and meaningful life.

This section of the book highlights information on and illuminates how to use your gifts and talents in a meaningful way to amplify your relational strengths.

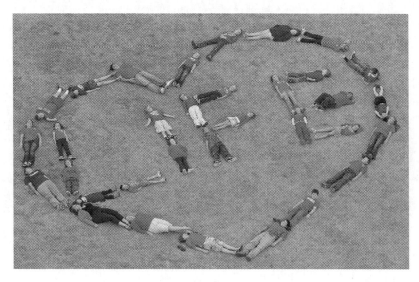

Kids from school in Black Hills of South Dakota
forming "I love life" heart, with photograph taken
from helicopter during "Red Ribbon Week"

Chapter 3

Celebrating Your Intelligence

*It's not that I'm so smart, it's just that
I stay with problems longer.*

—Albert Einstein

I began my career in psychology by administering numerous intelligence tests. The assessments were considered to be a reliable and valid measure of one's aptitude that would likely predict present and future academic and employment success. The assessments did seem to be a reasonably good measure of memory and problem solving, now referred to as a crystallized and fluid intelligence. However, something felt intuitively unjust about these assessments, which seemed to fail to measure important traits, knowledge, and skills needed to flourish in life. I now realize these assessments did not measure the test taker's social skills, emotional maturity, common sense, or strength of character. I remember one question from an IQ test that asked a youngster, "Where does bacon come from?" I remember one engaging and socially skilled young student who responded, "A grocery store." Unfortunately, that was not the correct response, which of course was from a pig. His response and other reasonable answers actually decreased his overall intelligence score. However, who was I to question these tools that were held in such high esteem by many prominent psychologists and educators?

Do you believe you are gifted intellectually?

Thankfully, Dr. Howard Gardner, who was a trailblazer in intelligence and much more credible than I, began to dispute equating intelligence with an IQ score from an assessment. His research and developing theories about intelligence expanded the notion that intelligence is so much more than an IQ score, which put so much emphasis on one's ability to remember words and solve problems. There are many domains that exist in various cultures to help one reach important goals (Gardner 2011). There is a growing body of evidence that there are at least eight or nine domains of intelligence and we all are proficient to some extent in each. No two individuals are the same. In fact, not even identical twins possess the same profile of intelligence (Anchor 2013).

Becoming more intelligent is not necessarily the goal of education. Rather, education serves as a facilitating force that allows us to develop greater character and competence, which lead to meaningful endeavors including work. Dr. Gardner's main interest is to better value and measure interpersonal intelligence, which deeply impacts the way you work with a group of peers rather than how many answers you get correct on a multiple-choice examination. The future will likely add additional domains of intelligence that we believe exist yet are difficult to measure. Our knowledge regarding intelligence will likely broaden in the near future (Gardner 2011).

If you were not placed in a gifted program, what intelligences do you utilize when you produce quality results? For instance, do you have a sensitivity to spoken and written language referred to as linguistic intelligence? Can you easily analyze problems analytically and enjoy math and science, traits related to possessing a high degree of logical-mathematical intelligence? Do you gravitate toward musical intelligence, where you possess developed skills in performance, composition, and appreciation of musical patterns? Are you incredibly coordinated with your bodily movements and can use your mind and body to excel in sports, dance, and other activities that necessitate whole body movement? Do you readily recognize patters of wide spaces and confined areas and easily find your way through mazes or read maps to provide the appropriate direction based on viewing the entire lay of the land, relying on your special intelligence? Do people find you very approachable and tell you their life challenges because of your interpersonal intelligence? They realize you can easily express your true self and are keenly perceptive, possess a high degree of empathy and compassion, and radiate positive energy to others, thus being encouraging. Can you easily self-evaluate and understand yourself as well as others, which gives you an intrapersonal ability to help regulate your life and that of others? Can you easily navigate your way through nature and the outdoors and easily recognize features of the environment with your naturalistic talents (Gardner 2011)?

There are additional types of intelligence that exist, but they are just too hard to measure, such as a spiritual or moral intelligence (don't worry; I can write a sequel to this book if you find it helpful). Regardless, the good news is that you have a unique blend of intelligences. The bad news is that in certain cultures, some types of intelligences are held in high esteem and may create an unfair bias in our educational and work environments. You can clearly see why being an educator is challenging, especially when politicians try to set a one-size-fits-all standard.

Do you believe you can produce do something extraordinary?

Writing a book is humbling, and I catch myself occasionally wondering if I am worthy or smart enough to represent a person thriving in life regardless of the fact that I am a tenured professor, licensed psychologist, and national workshop presenter. There is still a voice inside of me that creeps into my consciousness: "If they really knew me, they would know that I do not always subscribe to my own wisdom." There is another voice that has taken me more than fifty years to subdue. It's the voice of my situational self-doubt. I have been quietly observing the world all my life, have conducted over five thousand counseling sessions, and have a unique sense of perception, intuition, and creativity. I have had numerous evaluations from teaching more than 150 graduate classes and conducting numerous workshops around the United States, and beyond that, I have significant pragmatic wisdom that is appreciated, and a dry sense of humor to boot. I feel good about my life regardless of some bumps on my path, including almost getting held back in the third grade

My life may not be as compelling as some of those showered with fame and money, but I would like to provide a context for my motive in writing this book for you. I was fortunate to be raised by two loving parents, who showered me with love and encouragement. They did have high expectations of me when it came to making the right decisions, and they had always hoped I'd value higher education. Conversely, I was the last born and knew how to play the "compliant good boy" role that loosened my parents' expectations of me, and I admit it, it was probably unfair and perhaps a little frustrating for my older sister and brother, who viewed me as pampered and spoiled because of my sensitivity.

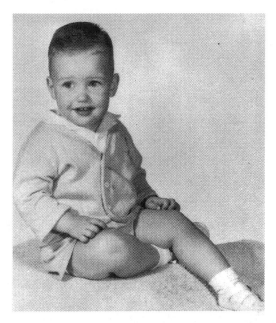

Sorry—I am going for the "ah, he is so cute" response.

Is your past really dead and gone?

My early school years were full of excitement, hope, and insecurity. I started school believing I could learn anything and soon found out that maybe I was just average or slightly above. In my earlier academic years, I too often struggled to remember details (probably still do—just ask my wife), especially when small things are perceived to be insignificant. I struggled to focus on drawing inside the lines and remember feeling like I had to read at a slower pace to catch the details that might be on the test, although I could grasp the major themes quite easily. My grades were somewhat adequate but significantly improved later in life when understanding theories and using my creativity seemed to matter. My early school performance was also exacerbated by daydreaming about how to walk or ride my bike safely home without being noticed by our school bully, who usually chose someone at random to pummel every week until high school, when I believe he dropped out. More on that later.

I am sure most of my teachers were excellent. However, it was clear who the early academic stars were based on what reading level you were put in: Winston (top students), Allyn and Bacon (average students), and Ginn (the slowest students). Most of the students were probably more resilient and less sensitive than I was. My memories are somewhat vague and perhaps embellished. I can remember pooping in my pants in kindergarten and pretending everything was fine, until I successfully made it through the half-day and walked slowly home (sorry about the imagery, and at least it didn't happen in middle school). I, unfortunately, remember Ms. Not-so-nice, a fourth-grade teacher who would literally grab kids in the back of the head when they were acting out, especially during recess (obviously not her favorite part of the school day). She then would take any hair that she was able to pull out and put it in an envelope with the student's name on it. I heard that she would then use her evidence of misbehavior at parent-teacher conferences, which frightened me.

My parents, Dar and Jo Britzman, with my children when they were younger. I know I am truly blessed!

How has adversity helped you to develop strong convictions?

I seemed to turn the corner to achieve academic meritocracy in the fourth grade, despite a terrible incident on the playground. The school bully, whom I will call Dennis, punched me in the face while I tried to mediate a fight between him and my friend Telly, who emigrated from Greece. I cried in front of everyone at the playground and then had to sit in class for the rest of the day with a black-and-blue eye. The bully, which I don't even think was the word back then, tormented me from the second grade until the eighth grade. Dennis typically would pick at least one kid a week for a beating. A few of the best athletes put up a good fight, but Dennis was skilled with his fists and anything else he could do to create a bloody mess or knock someone unconscious. I don't believe he was the founder of MMA fighting, but he was a cage fighter without a cage way before his time.

I look back at that time wondering why nobody seemed to intervene with Dennis, but I am sure there were a lot of conversations among adults. However, I would have given my entire baseball card collection for a school resource officer back then. Thankfully, the fighting appeared to stop when Dennis jumped Telly in the eighth grade, and my meek and mild friend, who had a growing rage inside and would eventually become a stellar nose tackle on the high school football team, put Dennis in a headlock and pummeled him until Dennis dropped to the ground unconscious. The bullying ended, as many of the tougher kids found alcohol and drugs more compelling than academics and dropped out. Today, they would have to stay in school until they are eighteen. The last I heard about my former bully was on the news. His name was mentioned as a result of breaking out of prison and being vigorously pursued by law enforcement. They mentioned he was likely armed and dangerous, and that old sick feeling engulfed me once again until he was apprehended. I believe he is serving a life sentence, which still doesn't make me feel any better.

The good news is that my academic prowess slowly improved, although most of my middle school years are repressed, with the exception of experiencing an indescribable delight if Polly, Tracie, or Jackie said "hi" to me during the day. Puberty and acne do not make for compelling reading anyway. I did have a beginning notion, however, that I had a special talent for possessing a keen perception of others, combined with a compassionate spirit to be helpful.

This particular skill was never tested, but Dr. Howard Gardner, a developmental psychologist and former professor at Harvard who viewed intelligence as more than a myopic phenomenon, would have likely concluded that I was gifted in the area of interpersonal and intrapersonal intelligence. In laymen's terms, I have a unique ability to understand and relate to other people, and I'm skilled at assessing the emotions, motivations, and intentions of others. I am articulate, am able to see situations from numerous perspectives, and can resolve conflicts and develop positive relationships with others (Gardner 2011).

My grades steadily improved in high school because I could easily sense what the teachers wanted me to learn, and then I would spend the rest of my time playing sports. Yes, I also had a slightly better-than-average kinesthetic ability, which means I was a decent shooter in basketball, but only had a two-inch vertical leap. I was also an all-star baseball player. I had no clue what I would do later in life, especially after I tore a rotator cuff in my arm pitching three baseball games in a row in four days (drinking water in those days as an athlete was a sign of weakness, and the team I pitched for was called "The Arrow Bar"). Becoming a professional athlete slowly became a fading and disappointing delusion.

Perhaps I gave up on my professional baseball dream
too early with this fundamentally sound form!

What is your dream job?

I don't remember taking any career assessments back then. I know my parents expected me to go to college, which made sense after my parks department incident (more on that later) followed by another summer job that entailed building hog farms, where I witnessed a coworker saw off his finger and another get crushed by a rafter that fell on him. Two other workers got fired when it was found out by our foreman that they were trying to coerce me, the seventeen-year-old kid, to pick up a drug shipment at the airport. Anyway, going to college did not seem like too bad of an idea and my grades were decent enough, but my sense of self-doubt had not totally disappeared.

In college I thought I would finally be found to be academically challenged, but instead I thrived (studying actually helps). I could no longer slack off, try to get homework done in any way possible, and spend most of my time dreaming about making the winning shot in basketball if the coach would notice me eagerly waiting on the bench and rooting for our starters to mess up (sorry, Chuck). I did not have any contact with our school counselor in high school with the exception of asking where his office was to pick up my ACT score, so my career assessment process came from the equivalent of throwing darts at possibilities. Hmmm … professional athlete? Not probable, as I did not start for my high school basketball team, and my pitching arm went dead. My dad mentioned something about a great demand for hog managers. That was probably well-intended advice, but I am afraid of large animals when I do not have a hunting gun in my hand. I did think, *It would be cool if I were a doctor in something, and that would certainly make my parents proud.* Hmmm … medical school? Too hard. Perhaps dentistry, but looking inside mouths all day—not real compelling. I know, "How about becoming an eye doctor?" I declared preoptometry as my major without any knowledge until I met with my advisor and learned that I would be taking numerous chemistry, biology, and physics classes. Maybe these classes would be interesting, but I didn't take any of those classes in high school. Somehow, I dragged myself to those classes and managed to earn a 3.5 GPA my first two years of college. However, I rewarded my hard work and numerous hours in the library by leaving my favorite assignments for last—in psychology. I had a wonderful psychology professor, and I could not wait for class or to read the text late into the night. You know where this is going. I would change my major and join the ranks of the thousands of psychology majors, many of whom are on someone's porch right now delivering pizza, which is a worthy job and does involve positive reinforcement. I believe at least eighty caring individuals asked me, "What are you going to do with a psychology major?" Sound familiar?

How have social comparisons impacted your view of self?

There is an intuitive part of me that knew there was so much more to intelligence than just getting excellent grades and test scores, even though mine fortunately improved. Have you ever had a friend who did well in school but lacked common sense? One of my very best friends growing up—we will call him Jerry—was incredibly skilled yet humble in school. When asked how he did on a test, his obligatory response was, "I must have failed it." However, I don't ever recall him getting anything other than an A on tests and papers. Jerry never worried about anything, and nearly all academic areas were easy for him. He was, and still is, a great friend, but I still laugh about occasional lapses of common sense given his highly regarded intelligence.

I remember one time in middle school he forgot to write a paper and surprisingly wanted to copy mine. He had wonderful handwriting, and me—not so much. Anyway, he copied my paper word for word, and he received an A, and I received a C minus. I went against the code of violating his trust and confronted the teacher on her injustice, and she replied, "Oh, I must have corrected his paper when I was in a good mood." Wow! This was even after Watergate, so I expected a better rationalization. She did not change the grade. Another time Jerry and I were riding our bikes down the street, and I noticed he was headed right for a large tree limb that was in his way. This time his luck did not prevail, and he rode over the tree branch and was thrown off his bike. Of course Jerry, besides a little scraped up, was not seriously hurt. My obvious question was, "What were you thinking of?" Jerry stated, "It looked like a paper sack." I only wish the ACT test had those types of scenarios: is it better to ride your bike over a paper sack or a tree limb? Jerry could probably calculate the difference on a physics test, but in real life …

There are many Jerry stories, but a classic one is when we were nineteen years old, and we both shared a passion for sports. We had enough money to drive to Minneapolis, Minnesota, and catch a Twins game and stay overnight at a hotel nearby. After the game we decided to go to our room, where a rather older and unattractive woman surprised us as we walked through the lobby and asked, "Hey, boys, where is the party at tonight?" Jerry quickly replied, "Room 345," which happened to be our room. A few minutes later, there was a knock on our door. Jerry was perplexed and wondered who that could be as we had not ordered pizza yet. He opened the door before I could say something, and the woman from the lobby bolted into our room, grabbed Jerry in a private area, and posed the following deep question: "Do you not know that variety is the spice of life?" Jerry was so terrified that he could not respond. It took my interpersonal skills and about fifteen minutes to respectfully state that we were not interested in paying for any of her services. She finally left our room.

Jerry seemed stunned when I asked him if it ever occurred to him that she would be a prostitute. He stated, "No—I just thought she wanted to have a beer with us." Jerry actually is a fantastic friend, and despite his lapses in judgment and common sense, he is a wonderful family man and has done very well in his field of work, as he obtained an advanced degree from a very prestigious institution. I am sure he has some similar stories about me.

Do not believe everything you think!

Nothing is as important as you think it is, especially when you are thinking about it. We tend to embellish and hang onto negative thoughts like Velcro; positive thoughts often serve as Teflon and are repelled or dismissed quickly. This helped the human race in a more dangerous world; however, we are living in a time that provides many choices to promote longer life spans.

I would like you to close your eyes and think about everything that has gone well in the last twenty-four hours. Perhaps you can think about specific incidents or maybe just think about all the things you are grateful for.

Now I would like to focus on everything that has gone wrong. This can include but not be limited to irritating interactions with others, disappointments at work, all the things you are not looking forward to in the future, and so on.

Were you able to differentiate the overall changes in your overall mood? The power of positivity cannot be overemphasized, but it also takes much discipline to be more observant with your constant stream of automatic thoughts, intermediate beliefs, and deep conviction that perhaps somehow you are incompetent—or worse, unlovable. For instance, "It's cold outside. I cannot stand the weather in South Dakota. I should have moved to a better location years ago. Why am I such an idiot?" This negative-thought stream can happen in less than a minute but provide a foundation of negativity than can contaminate an entire day.

Our minds have evolved to attract the negative, as that kept us hypervigilant about possible dangers so we could take appropriate action. However, many of those threats are not rational, as there are not likely too many human-eating animals in your backyard. The old brain and its many functions to ensure survival is alive and well. Years of evolution have developed superhighways that can signal our frontal cortex to not only be on alert but also perhaps create possible worst-case scenarios that are actually irrational and unlikely to happen. For instance, how many things that you worried about last year became a reality? However, to quiet your brain when on alert with a fight-or-flight mentality, it's like there are gravel roads from our left frontal lobes to the old brain stem and places in the brain such as your amygdala (Hanson 2013).

It is not an event that directly impacts our overall feelings, but rather our perception and belief about the event. It is not uncommon to hear the statement, "This is one of the worst days of my life." Is that really true? Perhaps your flight was delayed, and then your cell phone lost its charge. I don't want to be self-righteous, but I can certainly find many things to complain about, including being tall and crammed into an airplane seat with the person in front of me reclining during takeoff regardless of instructions not to do so. Perhaps another perspective is that it is really amazing I can sit in a seat, albeit with limited leg space, and literally fly across the United States in five hours. I wonder what my ancestors living in the early 1800s would have given to trade in their covered wagon if they were able to do so. Perhaps they were more worried about being safe rather than feeling good about the day.

Your brain is amazingly complicated and powerful. New research discoveries with the aid of advanced technology have allowed experts to learn more about the brain's functioning in the last ten years than at any other time in history. Your brain is a remarkable instrument that can generate thoughts and behaviors related to love, respect, and kindness, but it also has the power to intensify feelings of hatred, criticism, and self-loathing. Many of us tend to embellish situations because perhaps it feels good that the worst-case scenario never happens and the situation ends in a sense of relief. We pay a significant price of chronic stress that comes with cognitive distortions such as:

"My future is bleak."
"School is stupid."
"I am ugly."
"This is the worst thing that could happen to me."
"I will never find someone I can trust."
"My cell phone sucks.'
"I hate my job."

Changing your negative self-statements is challenging yet possible. The process entails catching yourself when your beliefs become irrational and distorted. Once you identify your thoughts

immediately prior to unwanted strong and negative emotions, you can develop a consistent way of evaluating whether these thoughts are really true and valid. For instance, having your cell phone is frustrating but not typically a catastrophe. Sometimes just changing your behaviors can help change the focus of your thoughts and reduce the tendency to ruminate and make reality worse than it really is. Every choice, including your thoughts and behaviors, has a neurochemical consequence in the brain that impacts nearly every bodily function. The data are clear that self-denigration, perceptions of hopelessness, and sustained negativity serve as toxic waste, which often manifests in excessive depression and anxiety. Life becomes arduous, and each day may feel like total drudgery.

Unfortunately, our minds can go to the negative as a way to protect us from the worst-case scenario. You will likely pay a price for being hypervigilant to potential dangers that are actually unlikely to really happen. The ability to expand your positivity by evaluating the validity of your thinking and perceptions can be extremely effective in improving your psychological health and well-being. If that is too difficult, just change your focus on what you are perceiving in the present, such as a beautiful sunset, pretty tree, or wonderful smell, and you will likely notice your emotional reaction to change, thus experiencing a sense of inner peace and perhaps a sense of joy.

Life often brings challenges that one cannot minimize. Tragic events such as being assaulted, suffering from a traumatic natural disaster, or even losing a loved one can be extremely emotionally painful. The myriad of strong emotions in these cases necessitates dealing with fear and pain proactively, as there appears to be a natural grieving process that facilitates emotional healing. Trying to outrun or deny these feelings when life events are really bad creates a host of other problems that might manifest in other undesirable ways, such as suppressing your immune system, making you more susceptible to physical problems. The mind and body connection is intimate, and seeking help via the support of others, including professional counseling, must be viewed as a sign of courage rather

than a sign of weakness. Feelings of anxiety and panic are unpleasant and sometimes appear overwhelming. The real enemy is actually not your perception but the choice to try to avoid these feelings (Forsyth and Eifert 2007). The paradox is that the more we try to avoid difficult emotions, the more intense they often become.

Professional and licensed mental health providers often implement a process that encourages you to write down things you are thinking whenever your emotions become intense. Your feelings are explored, and you can begin to practice a myriad of techniques to calm yourself and soften negative emotions. Deep breathing and learning to focus on your present sensations can begin to slow your mind down so you can begin to think differently. Your emotions actually become your friend, which allows you to adjust your thinking and behaviors. Sadly, too many individuals turn to their default ways of being and often just try to grind their way through the day. The result is often physical, emotional, and even spiritual exhaustion. Short-term mood hits then become more appealing, but provide only temporary relief and deliver long-term negative consequences.

In our society we too often view being busy as the antidote to not feeling well. Ironically, when you do slow down, thoughts are stirred up regarding not being productive, which drives us to do more and more.

Being relaxed and peaceful is actually a very functional state, not a less functional one. Being overly busy and stressed-out is exhausting and distances us from our creativity and deeper wisdom, which help us perform better. Relaxation is a highly effective state, the most effective state, and periods of relaxation are necessary to function at our best (Lake 2013, 210).

Learning to relax and calm oneself is actually quite easy and natural. It typically necessitates focus on deep breathing and then focusing on what your senses are experiencing. Attention on what you are seeing, hearing, smelling, and feeling focuses the mind and leads to more peaceful feelings. You can then be more aware of

where your mind tends to drift and refocus with practice. Positive imagery that includes pleasant memories, experiences, and favorite places can also help to elicit almost immediate positive feelings that come with experiencing more inner peace. That is why meditation, prayer, visual imagery, biofeedback, or activities like yoga and tai chi are as powerful as the benefits of a more relaxed state. Resulting research findings are too many to elaborate on. The biggest challenge is just having the self-discipline to consistently give yourself breaks throughout the day to engage in more mindful methods.

Once again, recent research is validating what you already probably know. Success is fueled not only by realizing that you are capable and intelligent, but also by effort and a positive mind-set. A positive mind-set is similar to an, I-can-do-it mentality. Optimism emanates from viewing potential problems as challenges looking for solutions and trumping negativity and pessimism by cultivating a sense of self-efficacy. Fortunately, you can train your mind to have a growth mind-set that constantly looks for solutions. In contrast, a negative mind-set and resulting locked beliefs are the breeding ground for self-statements that often begin with "I can't ..." Sadly, many begin to believe the following:

"I can't do math."
"I have always hated science."
"I wish I were smart enough to play a musical instrument."
"I should have learned a foreign language when I was younger because now I am too old."
"I can never lose weight."
"I was not made to be a runner."
"There is no other type of work that I am good at."
"I just can't help myself."
"I am ugly."

I do not want to convey that you can easily change all your self-statements and core beliefs, but just review your life and remember the times you have overcome adversity or bounced back from failure.

My guess is, it likely entailed more of a growth mind-set coupled with effort. Another advantage of developing a growth mind-set is that it allows you to enjoy what you are doing. "Wow, I actually worked out for thirty minutes." In fact, you will likely look for other challenges. "I am a little sore, but I feel good about myself." You are not likely to be good at something without sustained effort. However, try to shrink change to develop optimism. "I have my workout clothes ready to go, and tomorrow I will spend forty-five minutes at the gym." Your plan does not have to solely focus on physical activity. There are so many possibilities to enrich your life. "This week, I am going to …

> go for a walk."
> call an old friend and ask him out to lunch."
> sign up for a photography class."
> eat an orange, banana, and apple."
> hit golf balls on the range."
> research fly-fishing trips."
> plan a vacation."
> go for a bike ride."
> get a massage."
> try acupuncture."
> go to church."

Anyway, you get the picture. A fixed and negative belief system creates the feeling that you really know that you cannot change. Competence necessitates much effort and hard work. Dr. Chris Peterson, a renowned positive psychologist who sadly passed away recently after a wonderful life and career, stated,

> We all make choices, or they are made for us. As a college student, I worked like a dog and had nothing that resembled a social life. My good grades opened doors for me not otherwise ajar. I walked through them, if not happily then at least purposefully. By 30 years later, as a tenured professor at a top

university, I now have all the dog biscuits I could possible want. And I also have wonderful friends. Maybe we can have it all – just not at the same time. Bow wow. (Hanson, 2013, 69).

Ironically, you cannot help but change. Is the change intentional, or just a result of trying to get through the day? A growth mind-set is a belief that can be cultivated and is dynamic; it entails that change is always possible, and so much of it is in your control (Dweck 2012).

Our educational system will also change albeit slowly. In the past, it seemed like textbooks were the curriculum and the assembly line of teaching every student in the same manner was the delivery system. Passing each test was the primary purpose. A recent focus is to illuminate how each student learns, focus on personal and professional dispositions needed to thrive to meet life's current and future challenges, and create an instructional learning system where students can customize learning with the aid of technology to ensure requisite knowledge, skills and attitudes (Schwahn & McGarvey, 2012)

I must admit I am not the most sensitive person when it comes to others complaining that it is too cold.

The hardest aspect about my job as a licensed psychologist is trying to help via counseling people who come to a session with the following belief: "I want my emotional pain to go away, but I am not willing to do anything different." In fact, there are some professionals who have standing appointments with clients just to discuss problems with no action plan. This may be the recipe for sustained income, but not success. I have to be careful not to get irritated when individuals encourage others to talk to a counselor with the expectation that a focus on problem saturation will allow the problem to disappear. An old Chinese proverb states, "Talk does not cook rice." Improving your life necessitates more than a discussion of problems. You must be able to self-evaluate what you truly want and your willingness to make choices that are more effective. These choices typically involve a change in attitude and behavior. There is some truth in the motto "Just do it" (I hope Nike does not sue me for that). I do not want to convey that counseling is easy, as there are a myriad of factors that impact problems, such as brain chemistry, unhealthy environments, past failures, physiological consequences of numerous past choices, and so on. However, when you cut to the chase, life improvements require a change in attitudes and behaviors.

Mozart worked until his hands were almost deformed, and Darwin collected specimens almost nonstop from early childhood. Jesus Christ died on a cross to help others find salvation. I am not advocating that your life become incredibly unbalanced by some incredibly noble quest for improvement, but I don't become energized by constantly sitting in my recliner and watching my favorite football team lose again. You do not have to be a prodigy to just get better at something meaningful to you. However, accomplishments necessitate hard work and obviously contribute to the pursuit of the good life.

Kylee playing the part of Glenda in the *Wizard of Oz* high school play. This wonderful experience can be attributed to the help of many amazing and committed teachers!

Integration Opportunity

Do you believe you are gifted intellectually? Why or why not?

Do you believe you can do something extraordinary? If so, what do you dream about doing?

How has the past shaped your current convictions and behavioral choices in major life tasks?

What adversity have you faced, and how did it promote resilience and perhaps convictions to help others?

What is your dream job?

How have social comparisons impacted your view of self?

How do you become aware of irrational self-statements or belief systems, and how do you dispute and replace these maladaptive beliefs?

Chapter 4

Searching for Deeper Purpose
and Meaning in Life

**We must be willing to fail and to appreciate
the truth that often life is not a problem to
be solved, but a mystery to be lived.**

—M. Scott Peck

Spirituality relates to the meaning, purpose, and direction we take in pursuing the good life. Identification with a higher power—whether or not you practice a certain religion—discovering universal principles that enrich friendships, and becoming more engaged in helping others seem to be major components that deepen feelings of spirituality. It is common for many to go through life dodging possible mishaps and hardships, seeking the comfortable route. There is obviously nothing inherently wrong with hard work and adversity. Self-responsibility is an essential concept related to pursuing the good life (Oettingen 2014).

What helps you make sense of your existence?

Becoming more responsible for renewal necessitates becoming aware of our current choices, evaluating alternatives to make life more meaningful, and taking action by seizing opportunities to make healthier decisions. Interestingly, when you ask an elderly person what the most rewarding time of his or her life was, the response is often that it was when times were tough and he or she overcame challenges. Perhaps the greatest rewards for living a meaningful life occur when we apply our gifts and talents in a way that makes life more rewarding for others despite the many challenges.

A pastor told a new acquaintance that he was always welcome to attend church. The individual responded, "I would like to, but I really believe that churches are full of hypocrites." The pastor responded, "Actually, we have room for one more." It is easy to become self-righteous about acting if we know the answers for our existence.

I realize I am in dangerous territory when talking about this purpose, meaning, and faith. Please know that I am very respectful of anyone's spiritual beliefs and try to model my faith instead of being an all-knowing fanatic (I will also save you from discussing my political beliefs). I do hope and believe that there has to be some grand design and purpose to my life. I also realize that I am not intelligent enough to understand the meaning in life, but that will not let me stop from listening to intuitive inklings and observations. I do not apologize for being a Christian, but do have many questions and concerns about life in general and how others may interpret it in a seemingly shallow and cultlike fashion.

I should probably begin with my biggest fear, which is that very few people will show up for my funeral. You are probably thinking, "Wow—and this guy is telling me how to pursue a good life. It won't matter who shows up for your funeral because you will be dead." However, it is my fear, and I will hopefully use it as a healthy motivation to try to leave a legacy by impacting others in a positive way. That is not only the right thing to do, but the by-product will be more people in the pews.

How would a near-death experience impact you?

What helps you enjoy your present moments? Unfortunately, many of us do not become passionate about life until we have a near-death experience. The life crisis often jump-starts us to begin to ponder our own sense of mortality. One of my first summer jobs at the end of another high school year was with the parks department. My first duty was to clean up the deep end of the pool with the park department's rigged aqua equipment and an underwater vacuum. It was tough to say no to this task on my first day on the job. My nervousness was compounded by what my boss said to me: "Be sure the generator is always away from the water. A few years ago, we lost a young man who reached up for the generator switch while in the water." After hearing this, my immediate thought was *I'm getting paid three dollars an hour to do this?* However, I knew it would not be a good thing to say no to my first important task on my new job. I strapped on the underwater gear that was made by my boss, Henry, and headed down to the bottom of the pool with an underwater vacuum and homemade face mask with air pouring through a tube from a generator that was plugged in far away from the water. The deep end of the pool was freshly painted but had accumulated dirt from a recent storm. The lead vest helped me sink to the bottom very quickly.

I actually began to relax and enjoy the experience once I could see that I was actually doing a good job cleaning up the dirty bottom. The pool would look very swimmable once the park opened the next day. I remember pretending I was an undersea diver like my hero Jacques Cousteau, an oceanographic technician. I was underwater for over an hour and only had the last corner of the deep end of the pool to clean. It was a good feeling to see my progress, as the bottom appeared to be much cleaner than when I had begun. As I reached for the last corner to clean, I was not aware that I had used up all the excess hose to my air tank, which was connected to the generator near the fence on the pool deck. The air hose became tight and disconnected from my face mask. Immediately water gushed into the mask, inhibiting my ability to breathe and see. I remember telling myself, "Just stay calm and take your lead vest off and swim to the top." I reached down to the vest, which was secured to my body like a life jacket but was fastened around my chest with a zipper. I reached down to unzip the vest, but a feeling of horror overcame me. The zipper was stuck. "Oh, shit!" I tried again without success. Then I tried to swim up, to no avail with all the excess weight of the vest. I tried to crawl up the side, but it was too slippery. By this time, I had trouble holding my breath any longer. I began to panic. Water covered my entire face mask, and I was unable to breathe. My last-ditch attempt for survival was to try to rip the lead vest off, which did not look very promising. Unbelievably, with the aid of an adrenaline rush, I somehow ripped the vest off my body and floated upward. When I reached the top, I was coughing and wheezing.

Another parks department worker was supposed to be supervising me, but he had gone on break instead. When I found him, I gave him a piece of my mind littered with words that can be spelled with four letters. The crew laughed hysterically, thinking this was the funniest thing that happened that summer. To this day, I am still not sure how I was able to rip the vest. One thing was clear … my time could have been up at the ripe age of eighteen.

I did not sleep that night because I could not wait until the next day, like a young child eager to have fun the next day. I asked myself existential questions such as, "Was that a sign from God, or just the consequences of really poor safety procedures supervised by an older boss whose thrill in life was to make life-threatening devices like a homemade aqua gear?" I pondered these questions throughout the entire night, and the next day I was more assertive with my desired job duty of pulling weeds and mowing. Concurrently, I quickly began to plan my freshman college schedule.

I have become much more active trying to use my gifts and talents in the area of providing counseling. I personally error on the side of deeds and don't want to get too comfortable with the belief "saved by faith." My only real agenda is to help others and try to make churches more of a one-stop shopping center for human needs, rather than beautiful and expensive buildings that are unoccupied for much of the week. Providing counseling in a church setting probably has not strengthened my faith in organized churches. However, I also realize that my sample is somewhat skewed with individuals paying consequences from poor choices and hurting others. Their impropriety includes, but is not limited to, infidelity, physical abuse, alcohol and drug abuse, financial scandals, and other decisions that have been irresponsible or violated the trust of others. I try to be nonjudgmental of the person and try as hard as possible to help him or her determine what he or she wants and self-evaluate his or her current direction and plan for pursuing a good life. However, it is hard for me to rectify years of useless choices that have produced a myriad of negative consequences. Lily Tomlin, who was a great comedian and not a philosopher, stated, "No matter how cynical you become, it's never enough to keep up." I can actually relate to that and have to work very hard at not becoming a self-righteous moral person who has a negative view of human nature. In contrast, I believe we do suffer from the disease of low expectations, and too often, what we allow, we encourage. Saying that, I have made many poor choices in life as well, but many have been inconsequential.

How do you show others that they matter?

My convictions for being more proactive and helping transform churches and organized religion probably relate to earlier experiences growing up in a conservative church. I used to pray on Sunday mornings for my parents to let me sleep in (sorry, God, I apologize for that). However, they would like clockwork roust me, and I would have to dress up, put on a clip-on tie, and make sure that I didn't talk or sit next to friends. We developed our own Breakfast Club-like atmosphere and just tried to survive Sunday school, a church sermon that was almost impossible to make sense of, Bible stories that seemed like they happened over two thousand years ago (oh yeah, they did), and the worst religious experience of my life—three years of confirmation.

Becoming confirmed was supposed to be contingent upon sitting in front of a full congregation (it is not full anymore) and a cohort of eighth graders answering questions posed by my pastor. I feel sorry for my family, as I know I could have been exceptional if the topics were directed to sports trivia, but I did not have a clue about most of scripture. My only excuses are that the church was brutally hot that day and there were other confirmation participants that were even more nervous than me. If fact, four actually fainted during the process of intense questioning from our pastor. One by one I believe they were dragged to the pastoral office and given smelling salts or some type of strange treatment for reigniting consciousness. I am sure the pastor and leaders meant well, but this was not a spiritual reawakening for us. In contrast, we counted the days until we did not have to go to church again. I really feel bad for being so negative and perhaps I am embellishing how bad it is, but telling a group of youngsters that Catholics were likely going to hell, as well as un-baptized infants, was a very dangerous message for a church leader to convey, especially since most of my best friends were Catholic. I would spend many sleepless nights trying to figure out how to get them converted to the right denomination and ensure every baby would be splashed with water as soon as he or she was born.

I came back to church when I was marrying a beautiful woman who grew up Catholic. I knew that not any type of God could send my fiancée to hell, as she was gorgeous and he would have to be crazy. I remember the priest stating during our premarital lessons that almost all couples struggle in marriage around their first-year anniversary and this is a wonderful time to begin having children.

I thought, *Wow—I have not stumbled into that research regarding healthy marriages in graduate school.*

What questions do you have regarding faith that are difficult to ask?

I understand the skepticism of many, and possibly you, regarding faith such as Christianity. There are many relevant questions that I know my childhood pastor dissuaded me from asking growing up in a conservative Lutheran church, such as:

- Why do such horrific things happen to such good people?
- Are un-baptized individuals and people of other faiths really going to hell?
- Why are humans such a tiny blip on the history of the earth, and did God intentionally make all creatures, and if so, why dinosaurs? (Sorry—you now know why I was such a daydreamer and struggled not only in school, but also in confirmation).
- Why doesn't God eradicate the devil if one exists?
- Why do so many nonreligious individuals have extremely highly developed senses of morality, ethics, and enriched relationships?
- How much of your choice is related to free will or prescribed to you by a grand design from God?
- Why is the universe expanding, and why is it so cold and desolate to the point that stars will eventually burn up and it will destroy itself?
- Fear-based motivation (e.g., killing firstborn babies, heaven and hell, allowing the Holocaust) is somewhat primitive from a powerful and loving God. Why would God allow this to happen?

- Are near-death experiences universal, or just a complex consequence of oxygen deprivation during death and impact on brain functioning?
- Can we believe more in the Big Bang theory and not Adam and Eve? (I am not talking about the popular television show, so apologies to Sheldon and the gang.)
- Is it really necessary to have so many denominations that build big, expensive, and underutilized churches that are often next to each other when there are a myriad of social challenges in our own neighborhood and beyond, including poverty, homelessness, and fragile families?

I have many more questions, but until we find out more about dark matter, I'll continue to be humble regarding what I call my limited knowledge about challenging questions regarding creation and our universe.

There is a host of other questions and observations that make a credible argument for a designed creator as well.

- Something had to precede the universe, and it is seemingly impossible to create something from nothing.
- The Big Bang theory is really probably misleading, as it is really empty space that is expanding right now instead of superdense pellets.
- Is there a strong possibility of multiple universes that might have a past cosmic universe, such as a something that existed before our cosmic beginning (wow—this is getting too deep)?
- Why is our universe so orderly?
- Can we adopt Eastern religion, which pursues enlightenment instead of logic?
- Why is the earth and perhaps billions of other planets made perfectly for life?

- Can we be moral and truly love our neighbor without God's existence?
- How can we dismiss the life of Jesus Christ when there is so much evidence that it occurred not very long ago?

I can see why organized religion is struggling in many countries. Younger people are more empowered to make their own choices, and the freedom they have obtained allows a deeper discernment regarding "What is life all about, and if there is an all-loving and powerful God, where is he or she?" The older generation is probably more fear-based and enjoyed the routine of faith rituals. Many younger individuals are tired and see organized religion as sometimes an insurance policy for getting into heaven.

What can good people with divergent views agree upon?

Life, and specifically the American culture, appears so incredibly superficial, fixated on sports, movie stars, self-indulgence, and chasing short-term moods, that wouldn't it be depressing if that is all there is to life? We are not much more important than flies on a muddy pig (sorry for the visual metaphor), especially if there is no purpose or meaning to life except to exist and outlast other people. That would be very depressing to me. Again, it's hard to pretend to be all-knowing. Our brains have not even allowed us to figure out how our brains work (I just came up with that one).

I continue to hope good people can at least agree on some things. For instance, love, respect, peace, hope, and forgiveness help make our world a better place. We can also combine the principles of kindness, responsibility, integrity, justice, and freedom, which appear to allow us to better cooperate and thrive as human beings.

This author believes there is a God, and if you do not, perhaps we can agree that there is something amazing that designed our world and we can just call _____ the great unknown!

Integration Opportunity

Have you had a near-death experience, and if so, how did the experience impact your passion for life?

How do you show to others that they matter?

What questions about your faith are difficult for you to ponder?

What can good people with divergent views agree upon?

Describe a time that you advocated for an individual who had been marginalized, oppressed, or discriminated against by others.

Chapter 5

Nourishing Significant Relationships

All you need is love ...

—John Lennon and Paul McCartney

Our need for social support, love, and belonging is rooted deeply in our genetic makeup. In fact, when we make positive social connections, pleasure-inducing hormones such as oxytocin are released into the brain and not only help us feel better but also improve concentration and focus while serving as a buffer against anxiety and depression. Strong social support, including being married, not only has many protective factors that create a strong emotional and physical resilience, but also helps us on average to live longer and increase the quality of our lives (Anchor 2013).

Who do you rely upon for encouragement and support?

The best predictor of happiness is having enriched relationships and meeting the need for love and belonging. There are over 7 billion people in the world, and it would seem that developing social support and significant relationships would be easy. Ironically, just look at all the lonely people (my apology to the Beatles, but I had to include them in this book). Although we have intuitively known that feeling loved and developing a sense of belonging and significance are primary needs, the data are clear now that the number one predictor of happiness is social support. However, in a world of clutter, with so many individuals becoming a walking to-do list with e-mails stalking them, it seems more challenging to give other people time, attention, and affection. Technology is wonderful, but digital signals are often a form of detached intimacy and can never replace a deep and meaningful face-to-face interaction (some individuals do seem to have an intimate relationship with their cell phone).

What are your biggest barriers to expanding your social network?

Being introverted, shy, and oversensitive has been both a gift and a curse for me. I observed people for many years and developed a keen perception for how they are feeling, what they are wanting, and ultimately, the purpose of many of their actions (that is why becoming a psychology major worked for me). I was blessed to have a few very close relationships, including family and friends, growing up. However, it has always been very challenging for me to initiate a new relationship.

I spent much time hoping that someone popular would notice or even talk to me or the ultimate wish that the girl I had a crush on would ask me to dance at a sock hop (old word for dancing before bumping and grinding). Without assertive action on my part, I waited for a long time. Elementary school was the recipe for confusion regarding strong feelings for girls and how to become cool with the guys. I remember dreams (prepuberty, so don't worry), but had no idea what I should do about my crushes that lasted throughout every grade. We were notified that the girls were allowed to view a specific movie about sex education. I remember in fifth grade, a time of massive confusion and ignorance, when many of the boys held some type of mild civil disobedience about not being invited to a movie regarding sex education. We were finally allowed to attend, and I never had seen such foreign objects that I guess were supposed to be in the male and female body. I could not make sense of any of it. Little did we know that the education focused mostly on understanding how to prepare for menstruation. Of course, I did not let anyone know, and when an older neighbor boy made jokes about using rubbers, I would laugh harder than anyone. I really had no clue what he was talking about and thought a rubber was something our dads pulled over their shoes in the winter to stay dry from the snow. Anyway, despite stronger feelings and weird things happening to my body, I literally had no idea what all the body parts were intended to do.

I will quickly gloss over middle school as I don't want to retrieve that memory. However, my confidence started to slowly grow in high school concurrently with making the basketball team (albeit sitting on the bench). I had more male friends because of sports. I realized the more detached and cool I pretended to be, the more they wanted to hang out with me. However, with girls, I was in heaven if Polly, Tracie, or Jackie (wow—second time I mentioned these three) just looked my way in the school hallway, or better yet, said hi. The fear of rejection was so pronounced that I would not dare to ask a girl to dance even when the last song was "Stairway to Heaven" by Led Zeppelin. The lights would then come on after the dance, and once again, I stood on the sidelines watching the cool kids dance.

How do you gain a sense of significance and belonging with others?

My good fortune changed somewhat in high school when a really nice, caring, and popular girl named Julie actually became a friend. Well, she was actually everyone's friend and later became our homecoming queen, which is difficult when our high school graduating class exceeded 650 students. Anyway, I looked wild, with long hair and a mustache (impressive for a sophomore in high school, don't you think?). My look kept the bullies and burnouts away, but beneath my disguise was a gentle, compassionate, and anxious guy. Anyway, Julie sensed that I was safe and that I would never have the courage to ask her out or do anything else, so she spent more and more time with me and, in fact, introduced me to many of her friends. I believe some of the guys thought wow, Britzman must be pretty cool to capture the interest of the most popular girls, but actually I was probably a good buffer or diversion from their true boyfriends, who too often had another agenda. I was safe. Most of my friends were female, but I don't think they were ever interested in dating me. I concealed to my best friends that I was a guy who could get action if I wanted to—I just preferred not to.

I realize it must be hard for you to realize that I was
challenged to find dates with this look …

My love life continued as I actually had a few dates in high school but still remained quite clueless. I believed that the many women in college would be calling frequently and knocking at my door once they found out I was from the big city (Sioux Falls, South Dakota) and actually played varsity sports in high school. Well, it seemed like a long wait. The drinking age was eighteen at that point (sorry; we screwed it up for the next generation) so there were many parties to attend. However, each felt hollow, and even with the aid of liquid courage, I did not have much assertiveness to introduce myself to many prospective girlfriends. Consequently, I went to the library instead to catch up on the previous twelve years of being on academic autopilot. That turned out to be a good choice as I could control my grades with effort and did not dig a hole my freshman year as so many did once they experienced true freedom. (It seems odd that you needed permission to use the restroom in high school, but in college, you could literally make any choice you wanted, and many did with serious consequences.)

I for some reason wanted to stretch my comfort zone, so I interviewed to become a resident assistant my sophomore year and tried to have a single room all to myself (sorry, Greg—my freshman roommate—but your snoring was like trying to camp next to an airport runway). I remember being asked during my resident assistant interview what my weaknesses were. I, unfortunately, had no answer (I was so naive, as it was a great opportunity to say that I worked too hard or something politically correct). I also did not know what the word *proactive* meant at that time; it seemed like a sacred word in residential life. Anyway, I was rejected, but the assistant director of residential life was desperate after other interviewees were offered the position but declined, and I was hired. Why would anybody in his or her right mind want to be an assistant in a residence hall at a period in history when you could check in a keg of beer at the front desk of the dorm? Residential life was part of a complex and holistic learning environment according to my residence hall director (we knew it was really a place to sleep, eat, and party for most students).

However, my room and board was free, and tuition at that time was about $2,400 (no, this is not a typo).

I somehow survived that experience thanks to my residence assistant partner and best friend, Brad, who spent much of his time being the sparring partner of an Olympic boxing hopeful. We also decided it would be a good strategic plan to befriend the middle linebacker of our football team, and he actually enjoyed having our back and being the third floor bouncer. Another residence hall kicked every student out after they apparently broke the all-time record for kegs on one floor for one night (i.e., twenty-nine kegs of beer). The carpet was beer-soaked and littered with broken ceiling tiles. Our floor's only problems were an individual caught pleasuring himself in the shower and another student practicing target shooting down the hallway with a compound bow and very sharp arrow.

What are the most important qualities that you are looking for in a significant relationship?

That year I decided I needed a real spring break, so I signed up for a field trip to Key West, Florida, for two credits of Geography. I was recruited by a friend of a friend and rode in a car with three guys and one guy's girlfriend who graduated early from high school and enrolled in college. We left Brookings, South Dakota, early in the morning (thankfully we did not have MapQuest or Google Maps back then, as I believe it is a 2,037-mile drive). We drove twenty-eight miles before our professor, who was fortunately in some other car and who also happened to weigh about 380 pounds, wanted to stop for breakfast. We started making our way to Florida, with Blue Springs, Missouri, our first day's destination.

I was ready for supper, and we ate in the motel bar; apparently it was ladies' night. There were eighteen individuals on our trip, and one that seemed way too attractive to notice who actually came up and asked if I wanted her free drink. I didn't know my alcohol tolerance at that point, but this really attractive young woman stated she was from Sturgis, South Dakota, and was attending graduate school. I looked much older than my age with long hair, a mustache, and of course, my really cool hat. If dressed properly, I looked like a poor woman's Tom Selleck. Anyway, she was really pretty, had beautiful skin that was already tan, and had a wonderful smile and personality. I liked her a lot, and since she was the first woman who actually approached me, I thought I had better start developing a plan for being on my best behavior and marrying her someday. I do remember, however, a sociology class about marriage where the instructor would have dissuaded my choice, as he advocated dating at least twelve individuals prior to making a lifetime commitment. It sounded good in a textbook, but in reality, that seemed like a stretch goal (I am no Brad Pitt or Denzel Washington—for the younger reader maybe Adam Levine or Harry Styles). How would I have twelve different dating relationships? If I had the courage in that class, I would have raised my hand and said, "What if number one was the right person?"

There are obviously many details regarding my two-credit adventure to Key West, Florida, but the good news is that we all survived, I met a woman who would later become my wife, and oh yes, I received an A for the course. They no longer allow students the opportunity to take that trip because of liability issues, but literally I was very lucky. I do not want to convey that my three-year dating process with my wife went smoothly. There were obviously other guys interested in her, and I had to work hard to make myself a compelling choice.

How could Rhonda resist this nineteen-year-old guy?

A female friend once asked me, "How do you even know when you are in love?" This friend was the homecoming queen at her college and had dated many men, some of whom she probably regretted letting go. She was thirty years old when she asked me that question and really wanted to start a family. I sensed she did not have that special passion for the man she was dating. I tried to answer her question, but realized I did not have an articulate and meaningful answer. After our conversation, I wished I had said, "When you love someone, you cannot wait to be together again when you are apart."

I know I got real lucky!

What do you believe constitutes a healthy or unhealthy relationship?

We now know from research that significant relationships and marriages need nourishment in a positive climate of respect and affection (Gottman 2011). Feelings of sadness, discouragement, disappointment, frustration, and anger are emotions that naturally flow from daily life experiences. Although negativity is inevitable and even productive, it also provides an increased awareness of what is not working and may be used to prevent erosion of your relationship. The pattern of relationship erosion usually follows this path:

1. You meet, and there is a strong attraction.
2. Feelings of elation are combined with anxiety about whether this person wants to stay in your life.
3. The attraction is mutual and sustained, and you become married.

4. Inevitable problems in marriage occur as your lives become more hectic and busy.
5. You do not manage conflicts respectfully and proactively.
6. Resentment accrues, and conflicts escalate to a point where you no longer feel like you are on the same team.
7. You begin to withdraw and forget about the facilitating forces that were supposed to bind you together for life.
8. You begin to associate your partner with negative feelings and protect your sense of self by using criticism, blame, and threats.
9. You withdraw from your partner and try to stay unhappily married or expedite a break from the negativity through divorce.
10. You try to heal from the intense pain and feelings of shame related to the loss of the vision for a wonderful, lifelong relationship with the person you once loved (Markman, Stanley, and Blumberg 2011).

Marriage is not a panacea for all our social ills, yet it appears to produce social good. Intact and healthy marriages are a true gift to child and family development that extends across lines of race, ethnicity, and class. Policy makers interested in decreasing poverty and crime while concurrently increasing child well-being and raising economic status would benefit by developing community initiatives and programs to strengthen marriage.

What destroys a marriage? Is it a terrible sex life … extended families … finances … health problems … poor communication … few leisure outlets? Marriages are actually quite resilient; however, negativity has the greatest potential to slowly contaminate and ultimately destroy a marital relationship. The worst culprits include but are not limited to conveying that your partner is the problem because of some defect in personality conveyed via criticism. This is a very different behavior when compared to complaining about the behavior. Criticism frequently begins with "you always" or "you never."

Criticism is often followed by becoming defensive. This behavior typically manifests in counter-complaining or acting like an innocent victim. Accepting responsibility for a complaint is often a helpful antidote to soften emotional reactivity.

Disrespect and contempt are the most devastating and best predictors of divorce. Disrespect and contempt often involve sarcasm, mocking, name-calling, or belligerence; calling your partner a derogatory name is a recipe for disaster. Partners that have successful marriages are much more appreciative of their partners. Encouragement and praise are crucial.

Stonewalling is a form of emotional withdrawal that further erodes loving feelings in a marriage. This happens when listeners withdraw from the conversation, offering no physical or verbal cues after they are affected by what they hear. Ironically, acting like you do not care, typically, is accompanied by a rapid heart rate and blood pressure, which actually negatively impact your immune system. Being attentive and turning toward your partner is crucial to resolve negativity in your relationship (Gottman 2011).

Imagine living with your best friend for the next 15,000 days—even the healthiest and most compelling friendship is full of challenges … welcome to married life. Living your life with someone you love is more appealing than living a life alone regardless of the moments of adversity and stress. Marriage is an opportunity to share your life, dreams, and aspirations with someone you love who brings out the best in you. Marriage is one of the few life choices that will truly transform your present and future. Ironically, we live in a society that puts more emphasis on the wedding day rather than preparation for this lifetime commitment and change.

What would it be like to be in a relationship with you?

Undoubtedly, it is very difficult to predict what the rest of your lives together will be like, especially as you both will encounter so many life experiences and transitions. How do you know that you are compatible to live the rest of your life with someone you think you love, and have you ever thought what it would be like to be married to you? We all have our relational strengths and growth areas. However, when it comes to partners, most individuals tend to be flaw-finders rather than talent scouts. Happily married couples behave like good friends and handle their conflicts in gentle, positive ways. You should consistently try to be a talent scout and seize opportunities to share your appreciation each day.

It is simply hard to look in the mirror and take an honest inventory of your relational strengths and growth areas. There are many important factors to consider. To get started, answer the following questions and then compare your responses with your partner's to help you imagine what level of compatibility you and your partner may have.

Who has the stronger social needs?	☐ Me ☐ My Partner
Who has the highest need for order and structure?	☐ Me ☐ My Partner
Who will be the most satisfied in his or her work and career?	☐ Me ☐ My Partner
Who is more of the spender in regard to money?	☐ Me ☐ My Partner
Who is more practical?	☐ Me ☐ My Partner
Who is more likely to be the dreamer?	☐ Me ☐ My Partner
Who is more analytical and rational?	☐ Me ☐ My Partner
Who is more sensitive?	☐ Me ☐ My Partner
Who is more stubborn?	☐ Me ☐ My Partner
Who has more energy?	☐ Me ☐ My Partner
Who has a higher need for affection?	☐ Me ☐ My Partner
Who has a higher need for having sex?	☐ Me ☐ My Partner

Who is more creative?	☐ Me ☐ My Partner
Who is more practical?	☐ Me ☐ My Partner
Who has a stronger need to have consistent faith rituals?	☐ Me ☐ My Partner
Who will stay in better physical shape?	☐ Me ☐ My Partner
Who has more recreational outlets?	☐ Me ☐ My Partner
Who is more resilient?	☐ Me ☐ My Partner
Who enjoys children more?	☐ Me ☐ My Partner
Who enjoys adolescents more?	☐ Me ☐ My Partner

I need to return to my story. I did marry Rhonda on September 3, 1983, and I really, and I mean really, am fortunate. We also have two wonderful daughters, who are much more intelligent than I (and will be rolling their eyes if they ever read this book). Being married and having children was the best choice I ever made.

If marriage is not a realistic goal, obviously family, friends, and even pets can play a significant role in the pursuit of a good life and even make you happier. Recently, my wife, Rhonda, recently found me facing the computer at home and sobbing uncontrollably, which doesn't happen very much (obviously a guy thing unfortunately). I just had to take my thirteen-year-old yellow Lab, Sunny, to the veterinarian to be put to sleep. It was brutal as I entered the door and looked at Sunny, who almost seemed to know what I was doing. He gave me a look and reminded me that he still wanted to be loyal and spend time with me. The last word I said was *good-bye*, and then I burst into tears and was not capable of telling the veterinarian, who fortunately was fully aware of what she needed to do. I felt less self-conscious when I noticed tears roll down the face of the veterinarian, as well as her office manager. Sunny was in pain with his lungs filled with fluid, and he looked sad for the first time in his life. I don't know if dogs cry, but I swear his eyes looked moist. However, Sunny deserved to die with dignity and respect rather than choke with each breath trying to get through another hour of his life.

Sunny was the epitome of man's best friend. I used to joke, "I just want to be half the man he thought I was." He was always eager to see me and get some attention, and of course he lived to go pheasant hunting in the beautiful and peaceful South Dakota habitat. I sadly had a tinge of guilt because I knew he spent too much time lonely when I left for work.

Please believe me that hunting is so much more than trying to shoot and kill a bird. Rather, pheasant hunting in South Dakota has been a family ritual for some forty years in our family regardless of weather conditions. My wife, Rhonda, often asked how it went when I arrived home from hunting, and my response was typically, "Awesome. We had a great day, but I am so tired." She usually would associate such a statement with a day filled with deep and meaningful conversation and often asked, "What did you guys talk about?" I would ponder and reply, "Hmmm, do you have enough shells, Dad?" Although our conversations were probably not incredibly deep (that does happen when I go fly-fishing), our sense of closeness entailed fellowship and bonding that is hard to articulate. We simply enjoyed the peaceful ritual and quiet beauty of open spaces (no, I do not work for South Dakota tourism). There is some type of spiritual connection combined with hard work and feelings of accomplishment as we typically walk between five and eight miles in tough cover (a word used for a slew of heavy weeds that were often wet). It may sound like a rationalization, but if it were not for passionate hunters forming groups, much of the natural habitat would be gone. Rooster pheasants also will kill each other for breeding purposes at the end of winter. (It was probably not necessary to add that, but I wanted to eradicate some ignorance about the animal kingdom.)

I really would not need to bring a shotgun along, as I am much more content to watch a dog like Sunny combine incredible instinct, skill, and relentless joy to try to flush a bird. I have fond memories of wonderful pheasant retrieves in water, snow, and deep weeds. However, you have to be careful to ensure a hunting dog is hydrated and does not get overworked, as they are so passionate, they will hunt until total exhaustion.

One day we did not see many pheasants, and I knew I needed to find a stock dam with water for Sunny to grab a drink and perhaps take a quick swim to cool off. I was hunting with my dad, brother, and nephew but made the mistake of straying off looking for water and hoping Sunny would flush a bird along the way. We finally saw a small stock dam with a tiny stream of water running out of it for a few hundred yards. Sunny bolted for the water. It did not look deep, but I noticed a unique stream that flowed out into a patch of dirt that looked dry on the surface. I began to panic as if this mirage of dry soil was some type of strange illusion and was really a disguise for a sinkhole filled with a thick muddy substance (professors in our agricultural science later described what it was, but I could not quite follow their deep knowledge of the evolution of this substance). Sunny was slowly sinking, and I burst into a sprint to try to pull him out and save him from going under. I grabbed him and somehow hoisted his eighty-three-pound body out of this thinly stretched muck that felt like quicksand. However, I began to sink. I don't know if my life flashed before me because my only thought was to raise my hands as I slowly sank farther and farther until this muddy substance created a body cast around my legs and chest. Wow, what a way to die, but there did not seem to be a bottom.

Sunny knew I was in trouble and kept coming back to help me, but he would sink and I barely had the strength of one arm to keep him away from me on dry ground with the other arm holding my expensive shotgun in the air. He paced back and forth and made an unusual squealing sound. He simply did not know how to help save me. This went against his strong desire to rescue me, so it was not effective. I also knew that the rest of my hunting family members were hunting fairly far away from me. I began to blow the whistle, which was my only hope. I was fortunate that my sinking seemed to stop around my neck, but I still felt no bottom so I thought this might be my last day on earth if nobody found me quickly.

Fortunately, my nephew Garth heard my whistle, saw me from a distance, and ran over to help. He calmly tried to grab my arm, but I could not move and did not want to endanger him. I told him to get Dad, who might have some idea how to help me with his vast life and outdoors experience. My brother Steve also approached, and even though he is extremely bright and capable, trained as an attorney and CPA, he suggested I should move my legs. I was not overly impressed with this suggestion as I could not, and besides, they were beginning to cramp because of the distress I felt. He then suggested that perhaps we had some twine in the car and he could wrap it around whatever part of my body was above the surface (i.e., head and perhaps shoulders, but not knees and toes). I uttered a rarely used inappropriate word, as a beheading was not my way to die at this point.

My dad, who was in his seventies at that time, ran over and gave me a look of deep concern when he saw me; he seemed to understand my perilous condition. He knew I was in trouble! At this point, a vehicle stopped on the gravel road in the distance, which seemed strange as we did not see many people at all on this quiet and peaceful day. We could see two individuals get out of the car and approach us.

A husband and wife walked toward us with a red wrap and threw it at me as if they had experience roping cattle. This was better than twine, and they wrapped it around the top of my shoulders. This approach seemed more helpful, but we had one problem. Sunny, who I never heard growl before or come close to hurting anyone, would not let anyone near me; he was very protective. However, Dad, who had earned Sunny's respect over the years, was able to console him. It took four strong individuals the next thirty minutes to slowly and gradually pull me from this uncommon muck.

I was covered with this substance, said my thank-you's, and barely made it back to my dad's vehicle. I took most all my clothes off (not a pretty sight) and plopped in the back of the car in my underwear. I could tell Sunny had a new sense of life and hope for our future going forward. My dad, who hunted all his life and is a tireless walker regardless of his age, asked, "Does this mean we are done for the day?" I was too angry, scared, and tired to respond, but I made it home alive. Fortunately, Rhonda was not home when I arrived. I tried to clean up the best I could and told her about the incident sometime later. Although it was extremely scary, the story has been recalled many times and perhaps becomes embellished somewhat.

What does Sunny have to do with a book about pursuing the good life? Well, we all have a cuddly hormone called oxytocin, and it has many positive benefits. It is stimulated with human touch, loving relationships, and yes, man and woman's best friend—a dog.

Sunny was a beautiful dog, a unique combination of sensitivity combined with incredible intelligence and strength. He seemed to live for affection and, of course, to run in any field, especially where there were pheasants. When Rhonda found me grieving, the only words I could utter were, "He would never hurt anyone." I wish more individuals had Sunny's loving nature. Our world would be a better place!

Integration Opportunity

Who do you rely upon for encouragement and support?

What are your biggest barriers to expanding your social network?

How do you gain a sense of significance and belonging with others?

What are the most important qualities you are looking for in a significant relationship?

What do you believe constitutes a healthy or unhealthy relationship?

What would it be like to be in a relationship with you?

Have you ever had a pet that you were fond of? If so, how did it impact your life in a positive manner?

Part 3

Someone once said that a vision without a plan is just a hallucination. Clearly, it is not enough to know what contributes to the pursuit of a good life, although it does help to be motivated and prepared for action by loving the good. Your life will ultimately be defined with the purposeful action you take regarding your quest to pursue the good life.

Pursuing the good life obviously takes more than understanding and fantasizing about it. The easiest way to change how you feel is to change thinking and actions. We can make human behavior extremely complex, but regardless what psychological theories propose, they all necessitate an ultimate focus on increasing the likelihood that you make the choices that produce desired consequences. Although issues such as free will can be debated, we seemingly all have many choices today that are within our control. In fact, we can stop the bad before it happens in many cases. You can literally savor what is good in your life by amplifying your positive experiences or even recalling fond memories.

Dreaming does not necessarily lead to doing. We can look at what we really want, however, and then determine an optimal direction and self-evaluate our progress. The good news is that new plans can be developed each and every day, and you can set yourself up to feel better. You can literally shrink change until you are successful in moving toward your goals. In short, movements beget change that often reinforces hope and confidence. We gain energy when we take action, and success does appear to breed success!

Most of us know what we should eat, and it is easy to want to lose weight when you are full; however, our true character is often demonstrated when we make the right choice even though it might be challenging or cost us more than we want to pay.

Change obviously necessitates effort. Knowing what to do and want to change establishes the foundation for change, but at some point, one must jump-start movement toward pursuing the good life!

Working with staff from Feed My Starving Children organization, meeting goal of packing 166,000 meals to be sent to Haiti

Chapter 6

When Adversity Strikes

**If the road sounds easy, you're likely
going the wrong way.**

—Terry Goodkind

I received a phone call that is every parent's worst nightmare. My daughter Kylee, who was eight years old at the time, was involved in an automobile accident. She was a passenger on her way to dance class in a car with our friend Chris, driving with her daughter Becky. I rushed to the scene on that cold December early evening as worst-case scenarios raced through my head. When I arrived it was quite apparent something serious had happened, as traffic was being blocked off by police and multiple ambulances and a fire truck were present, all with bright lights piercing the sky during the 5:30 p.m. rush hour.

I parked my car as close as possible and ran to the scene. A woman, who apparently knew me, stated, "Mark, I know who you are, and I believe your daughter is all right. We are keeping her warm in our van, and then she should probably be evaluated at the hospital after they take the others with more serious injuries." The street was barricaded, and media were filming the event for the evening news. I could see at least four stretchers taking individuals to the hospital and police interviewing the individual responsible for the four-car pileup.

Fortunately, no one was killed that evening, and Kylee turned out to be fine other than being scared and having a headache, which was disconcerting. Others involved appeared more seriously injured. Apparently, the high school student that caused the accident was distracted as well as speeding. He allegedly hit a curb with his vehicle and veered back into traffic, causing four cars to collide.

I was reminded that December evening how fragile life is. I was just relieved that Kylee, her friend Becky, and the driver and our good friend Chris were all right, as well as that there were no fatalities. It was crystal clear, however, that one bad choice can negatively impact many.

A few days after the accident, I reflected that I need to make every day more precious. You and I just do not know what day will be our last. I really like the idea of joining the TGIT club, as advocated by Dr. Richard Carlson (1998) in his seminal book *Don't Sweat the Small Stuff.* That is, "Thank God It's Today!" We could all rejoice and count our blessings, knowing that each day will bring a certain amount of wonder, surprise, and opportunity. Furthermore, members could focus on making everyone they know feel appreciated and reminded that they are valued. Catching others being helpful would not only make them feel good, but also ourselves. However, the true motive is because it is the right thing to do!

How has adversity impacted your life?

As a recovering master of worry and worst-case scenarios, discovering an upbeat and optimistic mind-set is not always easy for me to do. I am becoming more confident as I improve each day. I often ask myself, "How many of the things I worried about last year even came true?" I also realistically know that adversity and even a traumatic experience could be looming. All I can do is control what I can and let the unproductive thoughts and feelings pass through me and float away. I realize that I have been blessed with having desired outcomes when tragedy has been averted.

What do you rely on to feel better?

Everyone will face adversity, and I was fortunate to have a positive outcome. However, bad things happen to good people, and adversity is likely to lurk ahead of us. The only control we really have is how to invite enough stress into our lives to ensure we remain passionate about important life tasks and try to cope in a useful fashion when we feel overwhelmed.

Wellness is a holistic philosophy of life that includes promoting positive health by improving one's quality of life and feelings of happiness and well-being. However, do we really know what truly makes us well? According to Ben-Shahar (2007), the rate of depression is ten times higher today than in the 1960s. Is this based solely on the erosion of our physiology and attributed to poor brain chemistry linked to living in a faster-paced society? Seemingly, "a pattern of positive choices, or effective behaviors, characterizes a healthy and productive lifestyle, the opposite of regressive behaviors leading to less effective mental health and even mental disorders" (Wubbolding 2010, 20).

Stress will be a part of our lives for as long as we live. The critical factor becomes how we are able to manage it. Stress can be positive unless it exceeds one's capacity to cope. We need a certain amount of stress in our lives to not only survive, but also to thrive. However, when stress exceeds our capacity to cope, it manifests in many unwanted ways and typically zaps our energy and our zest for life. The challenge is to learn how to invite the optimal level of stress into our life to help experience greater levels of wellness and well-being. Learning to develop a positive attitude, putting problems in perspective, learning to relax, eating healthily, being physically active, obtaining enough deep sleep, and living in a place that evokes relaxed feelings all help to promote positive energy and help to provide fuel for your wellness journey.

We talk to ourselves throughout the entire day. Our self-talk impacts our brain chemistry, and messages are delivered in a variety of ways throughout our body. People who learn to have hope that they can control their circumstances and develop an optimistic view of dealing with difficulties reap many benefits and typically feel better. Many people successfully learn to become more self-aware of the connection between self-statements and beliefs and their direct connection on mood and energy. We can replace negative or irrational thoughts such as "this event is awful or horrible" with "this event is unfortunate; however, I can successfully deal with it." One of the most effective ways of doing this is to focus on our senses and try to imagine ourselves successfully overcoming adversity or perhaps remembering a place that is associated with positive images or feelings.

Physical activity is an opportunity to disengage from the grind of everyday living and work and helps you to relax, reflect, and think creatively. There appears to be ample evidence that physical activity not only reduces the likelihood of illness and disease, but also promotes greater energy and mood elevation. "People who exercise at least two days a week are happier and have significantly less stress" (Fredrickson 2009, 78). Exercise physiology is now advocating that we take as many opportunities to become active throughout each day as possible. Amazing physiological and psychological benefits can be derived from accumulating activity throughout the day. Safe activities such as walking, golfing, and gardening can have tremendous benefits on your overall health and wellness. Cardiovascular strength and efficiency can be accomplished via endurance activities such as swimming, biking, and jogging. Proper stretching can facilitate flexibility, while resistance training is vital to strengthen muscles. All these activities will help refuel your energy system.

Nutritional awareness is a complex young science that entails much speculation and confusion. However, it can be clarified by learning where food comes from, what its composition is, and what effect it has on us. Too often the focus is on dieting rather than eating healthily. The good news is you and I can make healthy choices that make life more enjoyable. The challenging aspect is that we often do more of the same due to deeply engrained habits and conditioning. We all know essentially what we should be eating. Fruit, vegetables, and lean meats are usually about 10 percent of what is sold at the grocery store and probably would not generate any profit at all without the numerous processed foods high in fat, sugar, and salt. You and I also know that we should drink plenty of water and be physically active for at least thirty minutes a day.

Most of us have been informed that there is no quick fix and loss of body fat necessitates eating a balanced, portion-controlled intake of daily calories coupled with increasing our activity level. To maintain this consistency entails discovering a way of being rather than a short-term shift. Wellness is a lifetime endeavor, and to experience its benefits, one has to learn to enjoy the process. Most nutritional experts agree that eating a variety of foods, including balancing calories with physical activity and encouraging yourself to consume more healthy foods like vegetables, fruits, whole grains, fat-free and low-fat dairy products, and seafood, and consuming less sodium, saturated and trans fats, added sugars, and refined grains, needs to become a lifetime habit. Our lapses, which may include binging on greasy burgers, french fries, malts, potato chips, and doughnuts, must become less frequent, or else our overall wellness will be compromised.

Are you aware of how your nutritional habits make you feel?

Would you intentionally put dirt in your gas tank? We know that even foods with empty calories can be consumed with extreme moderation. However, how many of us eat these things in moderation? To overcome the temptation, seek the support of significant others who can encourage healthy eating patterns and perhaps track your intake of foods and water. Also, be aware of old cues, which have been conditioned with poor eating habits, such as the reclining chair in the living room. Eat smaller portion sizes and try to concentrate on savoring taste, texture, and aroma of your food. Give your fork and spoon a longer rest between bites. Put down the newspaper and turn off the television and cell phone. Drinking more water and getting rid of empty calories at home will likely help as well. Too often overeating is related to an emotional state. We tend to blow it when we have feelings of boredom or are nervous, sad, or depressed. Unfortunately, unhealthy foods become emotionally nurturing and provide a perceived temporary lift. This mood-altering fix lasts a short time and typically leads to more cravings and feelings of guilt and shame. Attempts to reduce these feelings can include self-statements such as, "I'll wait until Monday to start eating better" or "What difference does it make now? I have already blown it." It is important to deal with our emotional states instead of looking for a short-term emotional lift. This is difficult, but possible when you come to the conclusion that great-tasting, high-calorie foods will not help you resolve your emotionally laden issues. A wellness lifestyle can help confront problems proactively.

Your quest for greater wellness is facilitated by finding the right blend of healthy eating, accumulation of movement throughout the day, and quality sleep. It is possible, although challenging, but when sustained, the intersection of these endeavors will improve your daily energy, mood, and probability of living a longer, healthier life (Rath 2013).

Creating a culture of healthy living necessitates being more vigilant about every choice and consequence. How can you fill your home with healthier foods, create an environment that ensures longer and deeper sleep, and ensure that you get at least thirty to sixty minutes of physical activity a day? Ironically, your life depends on it. Useful tips include just making small changes or shifts to your lifestyle. Remind yourself that small changes can lead to a transformation. Consistently engaging in a healthy habit for thirty days can lead to a lifelong habit. The following are recommended by experts in the area of health and wellness:

- Fad diets are the recipe for failure.
- Remind yourself that inactivity is actually a depressant.
- You are ironically more productive long-term when you get more sleep.
- Morning activity is optimal as it leads to a cascade of healthier choices throughout the day.
- Every bite you take of food either is a net gain or loss (e.g., vegetables vs. french fries; water vs. soda).
- There will be likely healthy and unhealthy ingredients in many meals, but if you were an accountant, which would be a net gain or loss to your overall health and energy for living?
- The quality of sleep can actually have a major contribution to either having a good or bad day.
- Too much sugar is actually toxic waste to your body and likely is associated with diabetes, obesity, heart disease, and perhaps cancer.
- Foods with sugar will become addictive, as it will create a short-term emotional high, followed by a craving, and creates a subtle addiction with long-term devastating effects.
- Sitting too much actually puts pressure on cells and can cause the body to accumulate more fat than it would generally—fat that congregates on your rear end.
- If the sugar content of a favorite meal is more than 10g, you want to find a replacement.
- Walking and stretching throughout the day really helps your overall sense of positive energy.
- You can usually judge the quality of food by its color (fruits and vegetables that have vibrant colors are almost sure to be good for you).

- Measuring the steps you take during the day may be helpful, and if you can average 10,000 steps a day or 70,000 a week, you will feel so much better.
- Refined and processed foods are probably at the center of the obesity universe.
- Family-style serving probably leads to really large portion sizes of food.
- Eating nuts, seeds, apples, celery, and carrots instead of crackers and chips and snack bars would help you lose body fat and boost your mood.
  (Rath 2013, Peterson 2013, Anchor, 2013).

Knowledge about choices that improve our health is unfortunately not enough. Good health and wellness requires discipline and responsible choices made on a consistent basis.

Fun and enjoyment are available to almost all, and so is the ability to seek opportunities to embrace enjoyment and develop a capacity for delight. You may want to look around and appreciate all that is right in the world. You can always enjoy the beauty of creation or take the opportunity to share positive experiences with someone you appreciate spending time with. You also have many stored mental photographs that evoke positive emotions that can be accessed at virtually any time.

We all have a need to make our own choices without unreasonable external demands from others. Some individuals view the world as possibilities and have an amazing ability to use their freedom of choice. They do not allow someone else to deter their hopes and dreams. Although life is not fair and there are many facilitating and detracting forces that influence our choices, ultimately we must seize the freedom to choose our attitudes and behaviors that are so intimately linked to how we feel. Freedom is often discovered not by avoiding bad feelings, but confronting them proactively (Glasser 2011; Wubbolding 2010).

Golfing in Scotland—a bucket-list experience!

It's perfectly normal to have negative emotions, and it is impossible to pretend they don't exist. It is possible to view unpleasant feelings as a warning sign that alerts you to make healthier choices. You can literally allow these feelings to flow in and out through deep breathing, physical activity, prayer, meditation, or any other way to experience and then let go of fear, insecurity, and anger. Try to catch your negative self-statements and rumination about worst-case possibilities and then divert and modify your behaviors and remind yourself of the things you are grateful for on a daily basis. You can also nourish your body, mind, and soul with healthy nutrition throughout an entire day. Try to focus on the positive aspects of your daily experience. Also, helping your neighbors is not only a wonderful gift to them, but also to yourself. It has numerous mental health benefits that can positively affect your life.

It is sad when bad things happen to good people. However, just as in past generations, we must keep hope alive and realize that almost all adversity can be overcome with a more productive attitude, perspective, and focus on what you can control. Lastly, ensuring healthy relationships with family, friends, and community is life's biggest predictor of happiness and sustained joy.

Stress in life is actually a good thing, as it motivates us to accomplish meaningful tasks. However, when it appears that terrible events exceed our capacity to cope, distress can take its toll on one's emotional, physical, and spiritual well-being. The by-product can be feeling demoralized, hopeless, cynical, and angry. These negative feelings are exacerbated if one has difficulty changing to a mind-set that focuses on broadening one's perspective and rebuilding.

The key to build your tolerance for stress and actually bounce back from adversity, trauma, and threats to one's livelihood is called resilience. This is a choice, but it is easier for some, especially when they cope in a healthy manner. In their excellent book entitled *Resilience: The Science of Mastering Life's Greatest Challenges* (2012), Steven M. Southwick, MD, and Dennis S. Charney, MD, advocate the following practical advice for becoming more optimistic, which is the fuel for overcoming adversity and jump-starting positive energy to elicit resilience:

- Try to remember that difficulties do not last forever. Take one day at a time and do not borrow problems from the future that may not occur.
- Where there may now be pain, over time good things will likely return.
- Keep the adverse even within limits; don't let it pervade other areas of your life (e.g., family relationships, etc.).
- Think of the strengths and resources you can use to help deal with the problem.
- Notice what is good, for example, acts of kindness and altruism are antidotes for stress, and it is actually better to give than receive.

- Rely on your religious or spiritual beliefs to remind you that there is very likely a great purpose, to gain a healthier perspective and give you strength to face your fears.
- Try to do the right thing and dig deep to find the character strengths within you, even though it feels like there is a cost for you to pay.
- Please remember that social support is the biggest buffer of stress and isolation is typically a recipe for psychological disaster.

Lastly, that there are things you can control, such as healthy eating, prayer, and meditation, and appropriate amounts of physical activity and then recover and sleep. You do not have to look at your situation from rose-colored glasses, as the situation is bad. However, please be reminded that most all individuals who cope in healthy ways overcome adversity within a relatively short period of time. Consequently, keep hope alive and ask yourself, "What are the opportunities for learning and growth today, and how can I be helpful to others?" (Dweck 2012). The key is, "Let other people matter" (Peterson 2013, 81).

Integration Opportunity

How do you stretch your comfort zone to become vulnerable enough to develop close and intimate relationships?

How has adversity impacted your life, and how have you overcome feelings of inferiority?

What wellness endeavors can you rely on to feel better?

How do you make a wellness lifestyle a lifelong endeavor?

Chapter 7

Finding the Meaning in Work

**Your pension takes care of you; your
passion serves the world.**

—I. K. Otchere-Asamoah

Discovering a meaningful career is exciting, scary, and quite frankly,
a huge choice point in your life. I continue to be amazed how many
hours of life are consumed by work. Furthermore, I must confess that
I worry for the new generation as they enter into a hypercompetitive
job market that seems to change by each day. As a result thriving in
life requires a comprehensive self-evaluation of your interests, values,
life experiences, and competencies. You will likely need to tolerate
ambiguity, as the days of stable careers with a thirty-year relationship
with a company appear to be rare. Furthermore, not too many jobs
entail obtaining a company car, country club membership, and
more-than-adequate health benefits and pension.

How satisfying is your current work?

Do you view your work as a job, career, or calling? Your answer
has profound implications to your overall satisfaction. A high-paid

banker who just cares about money and doesn't like the work will spend a lot of time being unhappy. A custodian in a low-income nursing home that views the work as a calling connects with the people he or she works with and enjoys helping others. Watering plants or straightening pictures is very meaningful when it brightens the life of someone else.

Career counseling is often challenging. I do not want to thwart dreams, yet there is a time when one has to be realistic. For instance, many high school students may want to become medical doctors, but also do not like advanced chemistry, biology, and physics and may not score well on their MCAT. If they are accepted, four years of rigorous undergraduate studies, three years of all-consuming medical school, and three years of a poorly paid residency with excessive work demands becomes the reality. However, some succeed and enjoy their work until you ask them how they feel about Medicaid and insurance reimbursement.

Saying that, I don't want to discourage you from following your passion and at least finding a direction that excites you. The job market will be changing at a staggering pace, and labor and manufacturing jobs are diminishing. It obviously helps if your passion and your strengths and talents are aligned with the evolution of new and expanding areas of demand, such as technology and health care. Fully understanding what you want to do with the rest of your life is nearly impossible, and sometimes future opportunities do not become clear until you reach the age of midtwenties and beyond. It is challenging to know what you really want to do when you have not fully put your skills to use in a variety of areas.

What gets you most excited about your job or career going forward?

Most of us just want to have a job, and then there may be a quest to become successful, and ultimately, you will likely ask yourself,

"Does the work I do today really matter?" My hope for you is that you find your work both interesting and meaningful. Furthermore, receiving a fair wage for what you do is also important, although the ultimate answer may be to really reduce expenses and focus more on basic needs versus an infinite array of wants.

In the book *Die Empty: Unleash Your Best Work Every Day* (2013), the author, Todd Henry, cautions anyone seeking meaningful work to avoid the "seven sins of mediocrity." These entail:

- aimlessness. Do not choose a career as if you were shooting a bow and arrow at a target blindfolded.
- boredom. This is typically a sign that your mind has grown weary of not researching possibilities.
- comfort. The love of seeking the easy way is typically the enemy of greatness.
- delusion. You just have to watch shows like *American Idol* to realize that some individuals have a distorted sense of competency about their dreams.
- ego. Are you resilient enough to handle failure and fall forward?
- fear. Feelings of fear thrive on the unknown when risk-taking is not practiced in a purposeful, intentional, and strategic manner.
- guardedness. When you choose to cut yourself off from others and refuse to become vulnerable, it will be more challenging to see your gifts and talents (Henry 2013).

Career decisions and transitions are relevant. An optimal process would be to first align your work with what you value. Making choices aligned with your values may necessitate observing what you would want to be doing regardless of income, which is somewhat paradoxical. You also would benefit by obtaining brutally honest feedback regarding what you do well. Every job requires differing competencies. You may need to have other individuals give you a valid feedback loop and ask questions related to the following:

- What is specifically happening when I produce quality results?
- What am I doing when I am most enthusiastic?
- What work environment brings out the best in me?
- Do I prefer to be surrounded with colleagues or work more independently?
- Do I tend to have a need for organization and stability?
- Do I have a need to bring out the best in others or solve problems?
- Do I have a thirst for every day being different?
- How much do I need structure versus ambiguity?
- If it were not for pay, what would I really enjoy doing?
- What am I engaged in when I lose track of time?

Career planning is an ongoing process that helps you continue learning, growing, and developing. The process typically entails the following:

- fully understanding your interests, values, skills, and preferences;
- exploring possibilities and opportunities that are available to you and fit well with your life circumstances; and
- continuing to clarify specifically what challenges you, what you enjoy, and what you excel in.

The process is dynamic and continues throughout your entire life. As a result, it helps to really know yourself. Conduct research on numerous careers. Make choices that get you closer to what you want to do. Then take action to find a career that utilizes your strengths and talents in a world that is changing each and every day.

Enjoying what you do requires a positive outlook, which is also highly related to your ultimate success. Please be reminded that even if school or tests are challenging for you, your IQ score is actually an invalid attempt to measure your intelligence and it accounts for only 33 percent of overall success at work. Your intelligence has to be augmented with three key beliefs (Anchor 2013).

What type of work is important to you?

The first is really believing that your behavior matters. If you believe a task is important, you are more focused and put forth more effort. You remember subjects or courses in school that just did not seem to have any pragmatic value to life. Your studies became more of a chore or job, with little satisfaction. It is not surprising that excellent educators and bosses explain the desired outcomes of learning new skills that broaden our vision and passion.

Second, a positive support network with individuals who believe you can accomplish important tasks is key. Encouragement and optimism from others is literally contagious.

The third crucial ingredient for success and satisfaction at work is how you perceive tasks. Do you typically view your work as a distressful threat or a meaningful challenge? I still have to admit that I too often get the Sunday-night dreads worrying about what I have to do the upcoming week. I then fall into the habit of snacking almost unconsciously to occupy myself. When Monday is over, I usually feel confident about the upcoming week and reassured that I do my work well and others appreciate it. Working out every day helps, but for me, my weekend time at the gym or better yet outside (during only five months of the year in South Dakota) really gives me an energized calm that I use to enjoy the present moments of the weekend and begin planning rather than obsessing about the upcoming weekly duties. I also seem to do better when I work in spurts throughout the day, and I even find a short nap to be extremely helpful (of course not while I am driving to and from work).

Commuting is really the most challenging part of my day. The sedentary routine is hard for me to overcome. I have listened to my favorite songs so many times that the pleasure is beginning to fade, and some self-help CDs just seem to define success with making money and becoming rich. Snow, ice, and below-zero wind-chills also make driving more stressful.

How do you deal with difficult and negative people at work?

I can almost predict that you also work with individuals who are extremely negative. In some work environments, it seems like the choice is to either collude in what is wrong with their life or be ostracized from their coalition group. Technically, we now know we have mirror neurons that seem to light up to environmental stimuli, including negativity or positivity. You may know of a person who, after a conversation, regardless of the topic, makes you just feel better. In contrast, there might be another person where you feel like you are living in Haiti and just fighting to get through the day. Negative individuals are truly toxic, but you cannot control their behavior. You can control, however, how you respond to them, or perhaps it is better to limit your interactions with them to a minimum. Negativity becomes like secondhand smoke in the workplace. Developing a positivity vaccine may entail starting the day by writing down three things that you are grateful for at work. Individuals who are saturated with problems are challenging, but try to get them off the topic at hand. It is probably not wise to agree with their negativity or argue with them; find a subject that they might actually enjoy. There has to be something going right in their lives, and then you can reinforce with positivity.

The following reminders may help you set yourself up each day to feel better. You may find these tips will help your satisfaction throughout the day as a student or worker:

- It is acceptable to be happy, kind, patient, more relaxed, and forgiving.
- Becoming stuck in a rat race of life is a choice and not a matter-of-fact, inevitable way to live your life.
- Be careful not to describe your day as, "Oh God, it was awful."
- It is not a badge of honor to describe how many hours you work or be completely overwhelmed.
- Do not borrow problems from the future such as, "I am going to be so tired next week because of my busy schedule."
- Anticipating tiredness often reinforces tiredness.
- Rest is not only acceptable but necessary and a healthy choice.
- It is good to remind yourself that it is not worth it to become frustrated.
- You don't have time not to exercise.
- It feels good to go out of your way to be kind.
- A solution-oriented approach is so much more effective than excessive complaining about problems.
- Complaining about the wrongs of the world will not make things better.
- Commiserating with others about the problems at work will likely make you feel more hopeless.
- Try to focus on the positives of decreased gossip about others.
- Every person wants to be appreciated and feel valued.
- Being respectful to others is simply the right thing to do and does not need an ulterior motive.
- Accept the fact that you have an occasional bad day.

- Your best ideas will probably come when you are relaxed and quiet your mind.
- Try to prioritize your daily activities.
- Examine your unhealthy rituals and habits and be willing to change them.
- Try to stay focused on the now and ask yourself, "Next year will I really care about this problem?"
- Being dead is bad for business (Anchor, 2013, Peterson, 2013, Carlson 1998).

It is challenging yet possible to develop the mind-set that today is truly a gift and make a commitment to happiness. All days are created equally, and your present moment is just as important as any future day.

Some people definitely just seem to be luckier in life. Actually, there is now a science of luck, where people who actually believe they are luckier than others seem to scan the environment for more possibilities that might reap rewards. Luck is increased when one is optimistic and seizes opportunities.

What are your towering strengths at work?

The job that makes you the happiest is likely when there is an intersection of what you are good at, something you find meaningful, and of course, something you enjoy. When you find a job that feels like a calling, it really does not seem like work. Rather, you often find yourself in the flow, and time goes by quickly. You lose yourself in time and actually feel energized. Your brain's resources have a crystal clear focus on what you are doing. It can be a tough zone to find, but very possible if you are appropriately challenged with your skill set. You are also more likely to look forward to the next day (Anchor 2013).

Why do some people succeed at work while their colleagues, many of whom are intellectually gifted, do not do as well? Daniel Goleman, who has a Ph.D. from Harvard University, contends that only 25 percent of performance at work can be attributed to sheer mental aptitude (2006). In a world where job security many places is tenuous at best, it seems important to know how one can excel at work and seek stability and perhaps advancement. Academic or technical ability is quickly becoming the threshold requirement to enter into a job. However, to become a high performer necessitates abilities such as resilience, initiative, optimism, adaptability to change, and empathy toward others. These attributes are often described as emotional intelligence and closely related to the possession of good character, that is, caring about how one's behavior impacts others.

Dr. Goleman conducted research with 120 companies and asked employers to define a successful employee. Interestingly, 67 percent of preferred attributes were emotional competencies, such as the following: self-awareness, motivation, delayed self-gratification, empathy, resilience, and excellent problem-solving skills. Emotional intelligence is not just about being nice or expressing feelings. Rather, it builds upon one's knowledge and skills and helps one become a primary leader of an organization by developing the ability for big-picture thinking, political awareness, confidence, and intuition (Goleman 2006).

Your unique passion, skills and experiences need to be unleashed to make a positive contribution to our world. If not, you may have to deal with the price of regret which can be incalculable (Harris, 2013).

Working with wounded service members' kids to promote
resilience and good character despite challenges

Integration Opportunity

How satisfying is your current work?

What gets you most excited about your current job?

What type of work would you find both challenging and fulfilling?

How do you deal with difficult and negative people at work?

What are your towering strengths at work?

Chapter 8

Making Our World a Better Place

> I am only one, but still I am one. I cannot do everything, but still I can do something; and because I cannot do everything, I will not refuse to do something that I can do.

> —Helen Keller

Pursuing the good life entails trying to provide every youngster with time, attention, and affection from parents and other caring adults so he or she feels a sense of significance and belonging. It is difficult to thrive in life if there is not a healthy moral landscape. This appears to increase the ability to influence positive attitudes and behaviors from both children and adolescents. Spending quantity and quality time with the child promotes a healthy, emotional attachment, and promotes the learning of important life traits such as cooperation, self-esteem, courage, and responsibility.

I realize that older individuals too often look at the generation being raised as a train wreck. For instance, when I was a child, we played outside all the time and never got bored. I could take my dad's old sock and make it into all kinds of cool things. Now kids are bored unless they have music blasting in their ears or are on Snapchat. You don't often hear about what people used to smoke besides tobacco (Google Woodstock) or the hideous racial oppression, violence, and issues that surrounded segregation. Of course, there are legitimate concerns about our youth and the lack of physical activity and perhaps growing sense of entitlement (I want what I want and I want it now). However, they are exposing themselves to a world that was created for them. The good news is that technology has made our world smaller and more accessible to becoming more culturally literate. This may cultivate empathy, and the best way to eradicate violence is to ensure everyone is fed and educated (don't worry, I know I would never win an election because I could not stick with desired sound bites).

Do you believe there is a growing hole in our moral ozone?

Spending meaningful time with your children, coupled with encouraging them to play, is a powerful combination, but perhaps becoming more challenging because of work demands and growing materialistic needs. Children and adolescents typically have remarkable energy levels. Unstructured play, especially in the younger years, is invaluable and allows children to both learn and renew by being active, creative, and spontaneous. The increase in energy appears to help them become more focused for daily tasks and responsibilities such as schoolwork. Play also helps kids learn positive peer relationships, reduces stress and tension, promotes brain development, and serves as a healthy activity that often aids physical activity and wellness. Rural life especially provides a readily available playground with an abundance of possibilities to have fun.

Just let me spread my wings and fly!

How can you interact with a child in a meaningful way?

Too many children, however, are being lured into sedentary lifestyles by being overly exposed to television, computer time, and video games. These activities seem to raise the threshold necessary for kids to experience long-term joy and happiness. Youth are being bombarded by provocative images including, but not limited to, violence, sex, and bizarre lifestyles, which just seem to change brain chemistry to want more and unhealthier images. This feel-good treadmill never seems to end in any type of enduring satisfaction and fulfillment. Furthermore, it often leads to youngsters becoming less sensitive to the pain and suffering of others, more fearful, or more aggressive (Meyers 2000).

It is easy to feel guilty for giving kids your leftover time and energy. Well-intended, yet guilt-ridden, parents so desperately want their kids to be happy that they often try to please their kids by being permissive or giving them an abundance of material things. Furthermore, spoiling kids with stuff reinforces the attitude of entitlement and wanting more, but yet ironically means kids are never totally satisfied. This sense of entitlement becomes very frustrating to parents who have worked hard for what they have. It also erodes good character development (Britzman and Hanson 2005).

As children enter into adolescent years, hopefully the stage has been set for them to become more responsible, dedicated, and involved in useful activities that facilitate development, as well as prevent temptations of peer pressure or the feeling "there is nothing to do, and I am bored."

To remedy their thoughts that there is nothing to do, provide youth with ideas of activities they can participate in outside of the home to keep them active and engaged. Most of our youth can easily engage in sporting events, club events, music, service learning, and faith activities.

Living in this era of time poverty and crisis, where parents are extremely busy, families must learn to manage life in harmony with what is most important. This necessitates open and ongoing communication. The family often provides the rudder that helps their kids hold to a course of responsible conduct even in the face of pressure from friends (Putnam 2001).

Consistent family meetings can help provide an anchor in the choppy water of life. Although it is optimal to develop this ritual when kids are young, it is never too late, and even teenagers can be compelled to attend if they feel appreciated and heard and are given some ownership for important family decisions.

The goals of a family meeting include acknowledging appreciations, preventing problems, and learning more about each other's feelings and expectations. Family meetings can also help organize the family's busy schedule.

My wife guiding Kylee and Ali down the right path …

You can create your own agenda tailored to your family's needs; however, the following can serve as a guideline:

1. Begin with appreciations and review times during the week when each youngster made a positive contribution to the welfare of the family.

2. Review and negotiate rules and consequences, allowing family members to provide input. Although the final decision will come from the parents, it is good to encourage a democratic atmosphere so that kids are prepared to thrive once they leave home.

3. Review the weekly schedule, as well as long-term planning. Ensure that important items (e.g., faith rituals, chores, leisure time) are preserved and take priority over less important things.

4. You may provide a weekly or monthly spending allowance to teach your kids about personal finance. You do not need to reward kids by paying them for chores. However, it is good to let them have some responsibility for buying clothes,

school supplies, and so on so that they are fiscally responsible at a later age.

5. You might conclude your family meeting by discussing how you can take control of any stressors or reach out to others in need.

Some rules of a family meeting include:

*   Be respectful of individual needs. For example, do not have a family meeting close to mealtime or bedtime. Turn the television and phone off during the meeting.
*   Every family member is invited.
*   Communication must be positive. There is to be no name-calling or yelling. Each member must show respect to everybody else.
*   Family meetings are not a place to lecture. They are a place to discuss.
*   Family members should try to see each other's point of view. Try not to be judgmental.
*   The meetings should focus on family strengths and positive aspects of family life. It should be a time of positive problem solving, not a gripe session.

Parents are the primary influence on their children's attitudes and behaviors. The value of family activities cannot be overstated. Children and teenagers need to feel that they have a place in their families where they can be loved unconditionally, yet are expected to contribute to the welfare of others, including parents, siblings, friends, and community members.

Too many youngsters attribute poor choices to feeling bored. If kids do not have someone to share their worries, hopes, and dreams with, they will often seek other avenues for fulfillment. Constructive use of time clearly involves shared activities that provide parents and children an atmosphere to work together and develop a mutual admiration and respect for each other. It is often when you engage in the most meaningful conversations, which strengthen relationships. Furthermore, activities involving grandparents and other relatives can also be very meaningful. Ongoing contact with extended family— children, parents, grandparents, aunts, uncles, and cousins—can help young people develop a sense of who they are, where they came from, and what they want to stand for.

Mindsight is a term coined by Dr. Dan Siegel to describe our human capacity to perceive the mind of the self and others. It is a powerful lens through which we can understand our inner lives with more clarity, integrate the brain, and enhance our relationships with others. Mindsight is a kind of focused attention that allows us to see the internal workings of our own minds. It helps us get ourselves off of the autopilot of ingrained behaviors and habitual responses. It lets us "name and tame" the emotions we are experiencing, rather than being overwhelmed by them. This becomes our seventh sense, which can contribute to our well-being. We can literally begin to make choices with our brain in mind that will provide a richer life by exploring the subjective essence of who we are, create deeper meaning in life, and better regulate our emotional responses with a sense of balance and appropriateness given the stressors, both good and bad, that we face (Siegel 2011).

More good news from the research front indicates that mindsight can be cultivated regardless of your earlier history through practical steps. This learned process can literally change the physical structure of your brain according to new scientific discoveries in the last twenty years. We are not only growing new connections in our brain in childhood, but literally throughout our entire life. This leads to better integration with the brain and helps us take control of our choices instead of just reacting in a similar fashion, which is often too emotional and sometimes even dangerous. This newfound freedom and flexibility is very exciting. It is becoming more common for individuals like yourself to state, "My entire view of reality has changed toward the positive." Of course, developing mindsight takes effort, time, and practice. A fancy word that you will hear frequently in the future is neuroplasticity, which describes our ability to grow new neurons in response to new experiences.

The area behind your forehead is part of the frontal lobe of the cerebral cortex, which is the most outermost section of the brain. This region is critical when you make choices regarding complex thinking and planning. Unfortunately, it is also the part of the brain that can suffer underdevelopment or damage with chronic distress or trauma. This is simplistic, but healthier choices—including reading, learning a musical instrument, or even participating in sports—can allow the brain to literally develop more emotional control, empathy, insight, and moral awareness. It is likely that individuals, and especially children, who endure detached and unhealthy environments have underdeveloped neural pathways. Furthermore, stress hormones that are released too frequently can literally contaminate healthy neural pathways and connections. This likely leads to more emotional reactivity regulated by the fight-or-flight response initiated by the old brain and structures such as the amygdala (Siegel 2011). This may seem boring (and I am no brain surgeon), but some individuals have brains that are like finely tuned race cars with no brakes. It is literally harder to stop and think about the right thing to do.

The brain is composed of many separate modules or faculties and continues to grow throughout your lifetime, and you may have a cluster of specific types of intelligence that cannot be measured easily via an outdated psychological assessment. Neuropsychology and new ways to research the brain are yielding fascinating results that will give hope to many who believe they are not intellectually gifted. The trend will move toward a psychological potential that allows one to process information in unique ways depending on what is needed in a contextual and cultural context to solve problems and create new ideas and products. Your intelligence, combined with a strong moral foundation and ability to respect others' divergent perspectives, will allow you to use your multiple intelligences successfully at school, work, and home, and in the community and society (Anchor 2013).

Mark J. Britzman, Ed.D.

How can you partner with educators to encourage lifelong learning and good citizenship?

Educators are often pressured to prepare curricula that rapidly change and improve your crystallized and fluid intelligence (e.g., memory and problem solving). These are important areas, and with effort you can likely learn many concepts that will help you become proficient in these areas. However, there are important areas such as your character, creativity, ability to work with your hands, interpersonal skills, and so on that you may be very gifted in that can never be measured by a test. Although you may not reap enormous benefits in school, the workplace will reward these skills, especially if you find an environment and job description that appears to bring out the best in you. Intelligence and character are both important. Societies run by smart people without a moral foundation can easily find ways to suppress, marginalize, and even hurt others, including having the ability to destroy the world.

We all want today's students to thrive in life. So, we must ask, "How do we want our youth to act when they reach adulthood, and how do our educational efforts serve that end?" Competence and character seem the optimally desired outcome for students to become life-learners and good citizens. Ethical issues confront us every day: being asked to lie for a friend, passing along a juicy piece of gossip, finding ourselves in a conversation with a bigot, receiving too much change at the store, using our position to take advantage of an employee, treating others in a way we would not tolerate for ourselves, being "creative" with work reports or accounting, and so on. How do people without enough moral or character fortitude respond?

How does entitlement erode feelings of happiness?

Many students and adults adopt a live-and-let-live attitude about behavior: "I'll do what I want, and you do what you want. You don't judge me, and I won't judge you." Decision making is reduced to risk/reward calculations: if the risk is low enough or the rewards are great enough, they can jettison ethical principles and do what they think will benefit them immediately. Many people who cheat on exams, lie on resumes, or distort or falsify facts at work are never caught. So the ethics of self-interest, at least in the short run, may seem to work. But the long-term risks are loss of trust, broken relationships, and loss of opportunities. Ironically, such a focus on self-interest is not in our self-interest. Furthermore, what we say and do affects others around us. We all teach the values we demonstrate with our choices, attitude, and behavior.

Dr. Gary Smit, in his excellent book entitled *Instilling Touchstones of Character*, stated:

> When we say someone has good character, we are expressing the opinion that his or her nature is defined by worthy traits, such as honesty, integrity, respect, responsibility, perseverance, and compassion. People of good character are guided by ethical principles even when it is physically dangerous or detrimental to their careers, social standing, or economic well-being. They do the right thing even when it cost more than they want to pay. (2013, 7).

Who do you know that just seems to seize opportunities to have fun and make the best of life? Someone I look up to is a person I will call Mike; he is an impressive high school graduate eagerly awaiting transition to college. He does well academically and is blessed with an engaging personality.

Mike enjoys playing music, including piano, bass guitar, and percussion, in the marching band. He also has a wonderful sense of humor and yearns to be challenged. Perhaps Mike seems like an ordinary, successful young man with a bright future. That is true; however, I should probably mention that Mike was born with no arms.

Mike would likely prefer that his perceived disability not be mentioned. He certainly does not want sympathy and takes any statement by others that he is somehow different as a challenge to prove them wrong. Ironically, what makes Mike most different is not that he was born without arms, but rather his amazingly positive attitude and the depth of his faith. When I asked Mike if there were certain things that he wanted to do but could not do without arms, he struggled with that question for a long time and finally stated, "I guess I am not real good on the monkey bars."

His sense of humor is another gift that Mike possesses. Sadly, he is stared at on a regular basis by others, and of course, there are children who are curious about what is wrong with him. At a grocery store, a young boy stated, "Look, Mom, he doesn't have any arms." Mike looked at his torso in shock and stated, "Oh my gosh, I wonder where I left them." He then proceeded to look up and down various aisles of the store to find his missing arms that he must have left somewhere.

Mike credits his deep faith for his attitude and views having no arms as an opportunity given to him by God to do something special. He also appreciates the fact that his parents have not lowered their expectations for him, despite his disability, or should I say, his unique gift. He views some of his peers as too "selfish" and wants others to appreciate the nonmaterial things, such as a close relationship with God.

I have to admit that Mike's positive attitude about life is humbling. When I become negative or cynical and lament about what I don't have or how much work I have to do, I remind myself that, "I want to be like Mike!"

The real test of ethical character is whether we are willing to do the right thing even when it's not in our self-interest or when making the right decision costs more than we want to pay. One of the greatest obstacles to being a person of character and leading an ethical life is the dominance of self-centered, pleasure-seeking values: doing what makes us "feel good," satisfying our passions and urges, and avoiding pain and discomfort at all costs. The morally mature individual finds happiness in grander pursuits than the temporary pleasure produced by money, status, or popularity. That is why educators are so often everyday heroes who earn their character stripes in the trenches of the classroom, often without notice or, sadly, recognition.

Student competency can be accomplished by better understanding how to use and improve knowledge in meaningful ways. There is a strong link between facilitating an interest in becoming a lifelong learner by being engaged in learning meaningful and relevant ways to construct knowledge, rather than just memorizing or replicating complicated tasks. This makes school relevant and learning much more fun, as each student can experience a sense of joy through using a skill such as reading a wonderful, albeit complicated, book (Gardner 2011; Lickona and Davidson 2005; Tileston 2004).

Although pursuing our own interests comes naturally, we must also make decisions that are ethical and take into account the interests of others and the long-term implications of our choices. Such a decision-making process does not come naturally. We have to model, teach, and nurture good character at home primarily, but also in the areas of education, community life, and workplace.

To understand the fundamental importance of character, we should ask ourselves some questions: Would we rather be married to someone we trust or not? Would we rather our coworkers or neighbors respect us or not? Would we prefer our children to be responsible or irresponsible? De we want a just society? Would we want to fly on an airplane whose pilots cheated on their training exams? Would you like to have surgery conducted by a doctor who faked his or her way through medical school? Obviously, we all would like others to have good character. But we must remember:

the best place to start is with ourselves, which always remains the greatest challenge.

In the last century, seminal thinkers warned of the erosion of character. Alfred Adler, the Austrian psychiatrist whose ideas have gained influence since his death, stated that, "social interest," a regard for the concerns of others, was the best barometer of mental health. Dr. Adler held that behavior is always purposeful and socially embedded. As a result, it is important to be socially responsible, cooperative, and altruistic, and to be encouraged to make useful choices to achieve feelings of significance and to belong (Carlson and Maniacci 2012). American psychologist Abraham Maslow concurred, stating, "The ultimate disease of our time is valuelessness." Lawrence Kohlberg, the famed developmental psychologist, also rejected the moral vacuity of values clarification and sought to help young people with the process of making ethical decisions (Britzman and Hanson 2005).

"If we as parents, educators, and community members don't solve this character deficit problem," wrote David Brooks and Frank Goble, "we are doomed to live with the consequences. If we think that teen pregnancy, gangs, and alcohol abuse, school failure, a loss of civility, the lack of work ethic and violence are the problem, then we are doomed to live with these symptoms" (1997, 120). In every relationship strong character is essential.

What are the primary attributes of your everyday hero?

Everyday heroes are often ordinary individuals that do extraordinary things in the trenches of everyday life. They often march into our lives without a drumbeat but leave a legacy that endures forever. Our everyday heroes somehow learned that living a life that matters necessitates being kind, respectful, honest, responsible, and a good citizen.

Dr. William Glasser, who became the founder of choice theory and reality therapy, stated that all discipline problems can be solved by not only having rules, but most importantly, having excellent relationships with each student. He said student problems are best solved by initiating the Golden Rule. This approach treats each student with respect by refraining from criticizing, blaming, complaining, threatening, punishing, and even offering rewards. Rather, the emphasis is on developing positive relationships and making learning interesting.

If educators are successful, the following eight strengths of moral and performance character will be the result:

1. Lifelong learner and critical thinker
2. Diligent and capable performer
3. Socially and emotionally skilled person
4. Ethical thinker
5. Respectful and responsible oral agent
6. Self-disciplined person who pursues a healthy lifestyle
7. Contributing community member and democratic citizen
8. Spiritual person engaged in crafting a life of noble service

(Lickona and Davidson 2005).

Schools need to create a culture that expects and supports quality and excellence, thus creating a climate and peer culture where each student can choose to put the following qualities in his or her world: self-motivation, controlling temptations, focus on effort regardless of results, focus on attitudes and behaviors, taking personal responsibility for problems, delaying self-gratification, believing in one's own unique gifts and ability, and striving for significance and belonging in a responsible manner. Pursuing a good life entails both character and competence. Our youth comprise 27 percent of our population and 100 percent of the future, and yes, almost all are gifted in some way.

Mark J. Britzman, Ed.D.

How can you help create a culture where character still matters?

Environmental awareness entails developing an optimal living environment that stimulates a concern for others. Developing a healthy community appears to be linked to an increase in moral behavior, and the benefits are often evident with loved ones, friends, colleagues, and neighbors. We too often minimize the importance of ordinary people who consistently try to do the right thing even when there is a cost. Everyday heroes earn trust by not talking behind someone's back, following through on commitments, telling the truth, having a high level of integrity, and being loyal in good times and bad. Our character is strengthened by being respectful. The essence of respect is to treat others as social equals and have positive regard for the dignity of all people, including yourself. Another trait associated with people interested in processing great character is responsibility, that is, being morally accountable for choices and their impact on others. In addition, of course, there is a profound need for love and caring. We simply must seize opportunities to bring out the best in others, including ourselves (Britzman and Hanson 2005).

Our interpersonal relationships are enriched when we truly care about another person's perspective and communicate in a manner that reflects a sense of caring, respect, and empathy, which promotes excellent communication skills. "Your odds of being happy increase by 15 percent if a direct connection in your social network is happy. In other words, having direct and frequent social contact with someone who has high well-being dramatically boosts your chances of being happy" (Fredrickson 2009, 34).

Kylee giving commencement speech at her high school graduation

I will obviously never be a Nelson Mandela, Dr. Martin Luther King Jr., Abraham Lincoln, Rosie Parks, or Anne Sullivan, but I can be inspired by their examples and have enough courage to make the world a better place, one person at a time, as well as enjoy the countless wonderful present moments. Self-acceptance and confidence are not purchased, but rather are earned by acquiring your character stripes in the trenches of everyday life.

I did have an opportunity to be an advocate for respect for the rights of others and our second amendment during a very confusing time in high school. There was an unspoken anxiety and almost panic that permeated our high school climate from an unknown source. Apparently, two high school male seniors, who happened to be gay, notified school officials that they would be attending our senior prom. This was back in 1979, and I am embarrassed to say that I barely knew about gay and lesbian issues at the time. I remember a trip to some basketball tournament where one of our older players was discussing a person called a "fag," but I had no clue what that derogatory and hideous term meant. I am embarrassed to admit, especially to my children, that alcohol drinking was common in the late 1970s. The legal drinking age was eighteen, and there was unfortunately not an emphasis on not drinking and driving. It was also common that many of the high school students, including athletes, smoked pot in combination with beer and shots of cheap types of liquor. I do not recall much, if any, prevalence of more deadly substances such as cocaine, crack, hash, or methamphetamine.

Regardless, I honestly did not care about two gay classmates going to the prom, but apparently authorities were very scared of some type of potential incident occurring. I also don't recall much violence in high school because there was massive attrition with kids who chose not to try academically or show up at school. I was stunned, however, when the media began talking about the issue of two gay males from our school, Sioux Falls Lincoln High, planning to attend the dance together. This not only made our local news, but was aired on national news; and the same week, there was actually a skit on *Saturday Night Live* regarding the prospective event. Perhaps this would have been a wake-up call for me if I knew the two classmates better, but it was a large graduating senior class, with over 650 kids.

The ritual in those days was to have a motel room with alcohol available (I am not sure what the parents were thinking, but I'd grimace if my kids did the same thing). I was shocked when I arrived with my date to the dance, which was held at a large downtown Holiday Inn. I was quite a passive and sensitive guy, but looked very wild, with long hair and a mustache, and I was about six-foot-three and weighed about two hundred pounds. Upon my arrival, a national CBS reporter who looked familiar from television stuck a microphone in my face and wanted to obtain my perspective regarding gay rights and high school dances. They could not have picked a more ignorant person, but I would have actually, even at that time, said that respect should prevail and that I did not sense that it was a big deal. Before I could speak, our principal, whom I did not even know because I guess I never really got into trouble, grabbed my arm and pulled me away from the interview. Anyway, my chance to be famous quickly disappeared (please be reminded that I was picked for Boys State because of my broadcast journalism skills).

Hang on because the experience deteriorated. Apparently, the school chose about twenty-five individuals, almost all male, to be followed by a law enforcement person with a gun. It didn't matter if I was sitting with my date, dancing, or going to the bathroom. A mean-looking guy followed me. Now I am at least aware of law enforcement profiling, but it was interesting that a white guy was apparently viewed as a potential threat for disruption or violence (I don't really remember hitting anyone in my life, but I did get hit from the bully and would have tried to take a swing at him in the fourth grade if I had not been crying). My two gay classmates, dressed in light blue leisure suits, were able to attend and dance, and nothing happened with the exception of tremendous media attention.

My knowledge about LGBTQ issues is somewhat better now, as I have had gay clients and friends who suffered enormously with the double bind of deciding to come out and disclose their sexual orientation and usually get pummeled with disrespect from family members, some friends, and much of society or stay in the closet and live a lifetime of self-denial and lack of intimacy. There are a myriad of other problems, and sadly, I later found out that one of my classmates who had the courage to attend our prom together later contracted AIDS and died way too early in life.

Okay, so I looked a little wild …

Seemingly, actions do speak louder than words, and many individuals who have tremendous character do the right thing very quietly without a drumbeat. Their skills are often groomed when nobody is watching, regardless of the consequences of being tired or stressed. There is vision for what they want from life and then an optimal direction for behavioral and attitudinal choices aided by continual self-evaluation.

Our essential goodness and inherent tendency to thrive in life can be thwarted by feelings of unworthiness and alienation. Unhealthy compensation for feelings of inferiority sets the stage for poor choices that provide a short-term respite from suffering but lead to long-term negative consequences and possible dependence on alcohol, drugs, shopping, sexualized behavior, overeating, and even perhaps grueling work—an addiction that our society too often applauds. Numerous self-improvement projects are sold with false promises of magically eradicating our problems. However, they are often illusions that allow you to play it safe, rather than risk confronting challenging feelings and the ultimate fear of failure.

Attempts to cope and just try to survive the day take us away from fully experiencing the present moment as feelings of worry, dread, and free-floating anxiety lurking everywhere we turn often lead to exhaustion and depression. We somehow believe we can outrun these negative emotions by keeping very busy, becoming our own worst critic, or developing a keen sense for other people's flaws. Life becomes a trance when we become accustomed to caging ourselves with unworthiness combined with dreading the future. The ultimate paradox is the more one tries to survive and play it safe in life, the more intense feelings of dissatisfaction become the status quo, producing a constant hunger for some type of distraction to protect us from risking failure (Brach 2004; Carlson and Maniacci 2012). The directions for getting back on the path for pursuing the good life become less clear. This book intends to respectfully remind you of essential choices that will help you pursue the good life that you long for. Fortunately, every moment provides us with choices, as all we have is the present moment. What path do you really know you want to take?

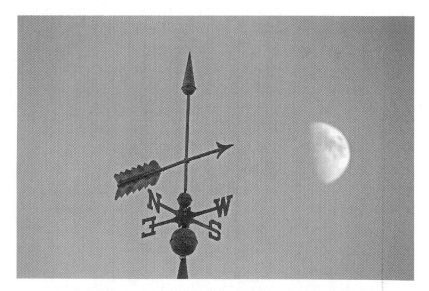

Your values become your moral compass!

There seems to be a plan and much motivation fueled by learning to enjoy the process and the present moments of unleashing talents and gifts in a meaningful fashion. The process of thriving in life will entail moments of fear and self-doubt. This is normal, and feeling anxious is not a sign of weakness. Our fight-or-flight response has been with us for thousands of years. However, our environments and threats to our well-being have changed significantly. In fact, the human mind has perhaps evolved in a manner to think negatively. Our minds are amazing, but can serve as double-edged swords. The mind help us analyze our world and generate ideas to thrive in life, such as the ability to innovate, self-evaluate, and be creative and adaptive. Conversely, our minds also have the potential to go to the dark side quickly by becoming overly critical and judgmental (Harris 2011).

Being mindful and bored at the same time is nearly impossible. Focusing on your senses in the here and now appears to eradicate the psychological smog that contaminates happiness and planning for an optimal future. Being still may provoke feelings of change. Ironically, fear is not your enemy and often is a friend tapping you on the shoulder, pleading for you to step out of your comfort zone. Expanding and opening yourself to fully feel emotions and contemplate possibilities just provokes stronger feelings. Please be assured that no one has died of feelings of panic. However, choices in regard to being scared too often serve as the breeding ground for bad choices inconsistent with your values (Harris 2011).

Accepting the entire array of emotions in life probably does not promote self-esteem, depending on its definition. Many conclude that high self-esteem, which entails a consistently positive evaluation of oneself and making and believing in positive statements and self-evaluation, is the correct path for sustained joy and happiness. How you go about increasing your self-esteem or defining it can lead to a distorted sense of competence or worse, a feeling that "I am better than others." We all have heard and may even know rock stars, movie stars, supermodels, and other famous people who are incredibly good in perhaps one area, but fall prey to an egocentric and narcissistic belief system. Denying one's undercurrent of insecurities can lead to an inauthenticity that will ultimately reveal itself and too often become devastating. Thus, I would like to make a case for the importance of self-acceptance, which creates a resilience knowing that things do not always turn out well when you stretch your comfort zone and adversity may strike at unexpected times regardless of your talent in one specific area of life. I am not encouraging you to discontinue positive statements, but rather to distance yourself from many of your stronger self-judgments that are likely not valid or helpful. What matters most is the strength of your character and courage to seize opportunities to make the world a better place, even if it's one person at a time. Pay attention to how this makes you feel.

I don't even need to own or be in this boat to
enjoy the beauty of the moment ...

Integration Opportunity

Do you believe there is a growing hole in our moral ozone?

How do you interact with a child in a meaningful way?

How can you partner with educators to encourage lifelong learning and good citizenship?

How does entitlement erode feelings of happiness?

What are the primary attributes of your everyday hero?

How can you create a culture where character still matters?

Chapter 9

From Surviving to Thriving

**Sing like no one is listening, love like you've
never been hurt, dance like nobody is watching,
and live like it's heaven on earth.**

—Mark Twain

Temperatures throughout the United States dipped below zero as the weather plunged into a record-breaking deep freeze early in January. I was very fortunate to make the last flight to my conference, which just happened to be located in Honolulu, Hawaii. My ambivalent feelings related to the desperation for renewal, fun, and freedom versus leaving family and other colleagues at home to struggle with the consequences of dangerous conditions. A person caught outdoors for any period of time will suffer frostbite and literally risk his or her life engulfed by 45- to 55- degree below zero Fahrenheit when considering the wind-chill factor. I would be attending an educational and counseling conference that would entail intellectually stimulating and inspiring workshops. There would also be ample time for a myriad of activities in paradise.

My experience was aided by an almost 100-degree temperature difference and a motel situated next to a panoramic view of the sun, blue sky, beautiful ocean, fresh breeze, and smells from beautiful plants and flowers that were actually flourishing. Individuals that came in all sizes, colors, and shapes appeared to be high on life. Kids played for hours on the beach; adults were laughing and active and seemed to be thriving with a rediscovery of fun and freedom.

Regardless of the indescribable beautiful setting of Waikiki Beach, there was a stark contrast of the majority of individuals who appeared to be healthy and thriving and hundreds, probably thousands, of homeless individuals and their few possessions lying on the ground seeming almost lifeless and barely surviving. I am not an expert on the homeless population, but I had a strong feeling of guilt every time I passed someone lying on the cement. I seemed to be paralyzed in my ability to help them and just ignored their mumbles for money, which just made it worse. Most all likely suffered from an untreated psychological diagnosis, which was probably exacerbated by alcoholism and a host of other challenges. In a paradoxical sense, I was amazed that they kept going, and I wondered what gave them any sense of hope or desire to continue to survive for as long as possible. The obvious warm conditions of Hawaii made it more tolerable; I have no idea how our homeless in South Dakota survive the winters.

Why do bad things happen to good people?

The world is not fair, and our ability to choose freely is overstated. We do not choose our genetic predispositions and our early experiences. Environments that are contaminated with toxic waste mixed with a lack of love, attachment, and security combined with losing genetics impacts individuals physically, emotionally, spiritually, and environmentally. A book can promote change and perhaps even transform a life. However, the essence of this book is to facilitate the movement toward pursuing a good life, which also entails paying it forward. Seemingly, we all have an obligation to make the world a fair, just, and compassionate place. I applaud all those who help the unemployed and know I should be more proactive as a social change agent with that particular problem. The paradox is that self-renewal is necessary to make the world a better place, one person at a time.

You likely realize that your life can be more meaningful, but there is no magical gimmick. If there were, 7,300,000,000 individuals (and counting) on our earth would form a very long line for the magical wisdom, or better yet, just one pill to swallow.

Pursuing the good life necessitates creating an optimal vision and plan for satisfying these needs on a daily basis. The best way to experience feelings of pleasure, joy, and sustained happiness is to ensure that our behaviors and thoughts satisfy our needs in a useful fashion consistently.

How would you summarize the ingredients for pursuing the good life?

I really do want for you to keep hope alive. Pursuing the good life necessitates continuing what is working for you and amplifying efforts related to the following well-researched ways to increase your well-being:

- having a sense of hope and optimism for the future
- developing a rich social support network
- challenging yourself in continuing education and work in an area or endeavor that matters to you
- developing compelling goals concurrently with developing a capacity for delight and gratitude for all you have in the present moment
- developing a sense of purpose and meaning in your life that is consistent with your values

- seizing opportunities to be altruistic and bring out the best in others
- engaging in consistent physical activity and fueling the body by eating food that is high in nutritional value
- taking time to be still and engaging in meditation, prayers, or any relaxation activity consistently throughout each day

You are benefited when you can take your wants and find a direction that gets you closer to fulfilling your basic needs. These needs likely entail receiving and giving love, feeling significant and empowered by unleashing your gifts and talents fueled by passion and fun, and having the freedom to do what you wish because you want to, not because of some type of external control.

The key is to do something different. The ultimate question is whether you can harness and mobilize the process of change to move you closer to your vision of quality life. Change is constant, inevitable, and part of everyone's life journey. Fortunately, positive changes can be set into motion by making just one shift in attitude or behavior. Please be reminded of the following: choices can only be made in the present. It is helpful to learn from the past, but do not be held hostage to it. Furthermore, accept the uncertainty of the future and focus on what you can control (Glasser 2011; Wubbolding 2010). The real test of pursuing higher states of well-being is to accept freedom of choice, especially when you do not want to. Your pursuit of the good life will be facilitated by the mind-set "With effort, I know I can do it!"

Life seems like a celebration when you are thriving!

Integration Opportunity

Why do bad things happen to good people?

How would you summarize the ingredients for pursuing the good life?

What are you going to do with the information highlighted in this book?

If you reread this book five years from now, what will be different in your life?

Chapter 10

Jump-Starting Positive Changes

**No man ever steps in the same river twice, for it's
not the same river and he's not the same man.**

—Heraclitus

It's obviously easier wanting to go on a diet when you have just eaten and are feeling full. The real challenge is making changes that are meaningful and sustained. The good news is that larger and more transforming changes often begin with some shift, which is commonly referred to in the contemporary research as shrinking change. Ultimately, the choices and resulting changes you make will likely need to be intrinsically motivating. "A well-established line of research shows that extrinsic rewards can undermine intrinsic motivation" (Peterson 2013, 186). Sadly, behaviors often stop or are extinguished when external rewards stop. That is why it is dangerous for parents to pay their children when they receive good grades. You may jump-start yourself by behavioral approaches and develop an elaborate reward system, but behaviors usually extinguish unless they become an enjoyable lifetime endeavor.

Mark J. Britzman, Ed.D.

How have you made positive changes in the past?

Have you ever wondered why it is so challenging to make and sustain a change? It is often so easy to identify that a choice is not working. Most of us know that there will be consequences for not putting forth effort in school, eating poorly, drinking alcoholic beverages in excess, or breaking the law, but many do the same thing over and over again.

I have to admit early in my career while conducting therapy sessions, there was a little bubble on top of my head saying, "You know what to do—just do it!" although my training was to be value-neutral and I was not to impose my values on others. This serves an important purpose, as it is essential to respect differing perspectives, lifestyles, and others' choices, many of which would be different than you or I would make. It also did not make any sense to me to discuss problems endlessly. I definitely wanted to understand someone's past and the context of his or her choices, but I would rather get a peek than stare endlessly at the past.

Most psychological and counseling theories were developed by white males with Eurocentric values. There was also a dearth of research regarding the effectiveness of psychotherapy, so many followed major theorists in a cultlike fashion. Professional counseling is very challenging to research. There are so many swirling variables that it is difficult to isolate exactly what is most helpful. Nutrition suffers the same difficulty in some respects when considering if taking vitamins is useful. Most of the research is correlational at best, but is not able to determine causes. For instance, are you feeling better today because of your attitude, relationships, physical activity, hope for the future, passion for what you are doing, leisure activities, or all of the above. (Or because you took your vitamins this morning, which somehow elevated your mood?) There are numerous daily life choices that can impact how you feel in addition to seeking counseling.

The fields of counseling and psychology probably underestimated the power of genetics. The argument regarding nature versus nurture's impact on choices is moot. We have learned more about the brain in the last ten years than in centuries of speculating. It is an amazingly complex creation, but does seem to give us numerous genetic propensities that are shaped by the interplay of life experiences. We also underestimated how the brain quickly develops and accelerates growth and continues to change throughout one's life span. *Plasticity* is a fancy word to describe the development and recovery of regions of the brain that continue to make neural connections as long as regions are activated.

What are the ingredients that facilitate human growth and development?

I believe the following knowledge will be reinforced as a result of future research endeavors:

- Love and close emotional attachment with others is vital for everyone to facilitate healthy development throughout the life span.
- Long-term stress, chaos, and abuse create stress hormones such as cortisol, which literally stymie or damage the brain's healthy development.
- Children need to be allowed to explore their world in a safe fashion instead of being reprimanded for touching, moving, and sucking things.
- Discipline needs to be instructional when a youngster has the abstract ability to link choices and consequences. A proper balance of freedom and structure is crucial.
- Individuals can have cultural values that differ and make our world exciting, yet relationship skills seem to necessitate universal principles such as love, compassion, kindness,

caring, respect, honesty, integrity, responsibility, fairness, and concern for others.

- Spirituality and faith can retain differing beliefs, but will hopefully help individuals become more proactive in truly loving their neighbors.
- Physical activity will become more important concurrently with reducing time in a sedentary place staring at a screen.
- Medical treatments including medication will increasingly become more effective at helping people feel better and relieve symptomology, but they can never replace loving relationships and healthy choices.
- Adults can helps youngsters by focusing more on effort than outcome. Developing a mind-set of "I can" with effort is so much more powerful than "I can't do it because I have failed at this before."
- Relational skills need to be modeled and taught early, including bringing out the best in others with respect, gentleness, and being eager to understand one another's perspective.
- Sex education needs to be taught in a factual manner; otherwise, education will be unfortunately offered via porn sites that will be easily accessible by young children.
- Career developments will necessitate clusters of multiple intelligences that will be related to what someone really enjoys doing, is good at, and has a market demand.
- Choosing a lifelong partner for marriage needs more discernment, skill development, and developing the ability to work through problems instead of just giving up on relationships that actually have potential to be improved and ultimately fulfilling.
- Short-term mood hits, such as alcohol, drugs, sex, overeating, and overspending, will almost always lead to undesirable consequences.

- Financial knowledge and willingness to live more frugally and simply will become more imperative, as debt can easily get out of control and lead to chronic stress.
- Successful aging will be contingent on developing healthy communities that use an older person's wisdom to ensure life is always meaningful and one feels significant.
- The world will continue to become more interconnected, and cooperation will be necessary to be good stewards of the universe.
- One must never retire from life and must keep trying to make the world a better place, one person at a time.

Any change is more sustainable when you have a firm and specific commitment concurrently with making choices that are intrinsically enjoyable. A mind-set that focuses on effort coupled with the encouragement and accountability of others also seems to be a facilitating force. Ironically, the encouragement to "just do it" is fairly good advice. Try to focus on smaller change, which has more potential to effectively begin the process of significant change. You can surprise a loved one with a nice letter. You can get out of workout clothes, put them next to your bed, and set the alarm for a morning workout. Once you are on your way, it takes more energy to turn back (Glasser 2011; Wubbolding 2010).

Change really requires just doing something differently. Just think about changes you have successfully made in the past. Making a new choice is obviously far more complicated when it comes to how your brain has developed and been programmed. The good news is that research is being conducted and finding new information regarding the tremendous plasticity of our brain structure. We continue to create new neural connections and pathways each day. The old brain, which some researchers refer to as the elephant or emotional part of the brain, has been modified throughout years of evolution. It seemingly reacts quickly to real or perceived threats and gets spooked easily. There are superhighways in your old brain that can signal a fight-or-flight response. The frontal cortex of the brain struggles to quiet these fears once the process is engaged. However, it is hard to quiet the old brain with the new brain because our pathways are like a lot of back roads; our neural pathways are still developing to effectively quiet our fight-or-flight response. Anyway, I don't pretend to be a brain surgeon (although I do have a friend who is a rocket scientist), but I do know much about motivation.

What can you do to feel more optimistic about making necessary changes?

Hope and optimism jump-start change. You can imagine where you want to go and what works. Change is also facilitated by knowing where you are going and why. This tends to quiet and relax the older brain, which generates good feelings. You can then focus more on effort (thoughts like "I can do it"), which is the mind-set you need. It does help, however, to change your environment (e.g., get high-fat foods out of your home, have your workout clothes ready to go, etc.). You can build habits if you can maintain new behavior for at least thirty days. Many people often find it helpful to state their goals to keep them accountable; others like to journal, and some do both.

Ultimately change happens when you determine a specific want. This ignites internal motivation, which is necessary for sustaining movement toward a specific goal. We actually have much more control over our life and choices than we realize. You can certainly use behavioral principles such as operant or classical considering; however, you ultimately want to make a change regardless of external conditions or consequences. Choice theory and its delivery system—reality therapy—focus on taking control of choices that are linked to needs that appear to be genetically coded in your brain. You have a quality world (i.e., vision of a good life) that serves as a picture album that represents a collection of wants and desires. Your quality world may be somewhat vague or blurred when focused on just trying to survive the day. Your vision of a quality world is dynamic and can be changed, which is the impetus for writing this book, that is, to identify wants that are known to have a relationship to feeling good and being happy. You may want to improve your significant relationships, expand your support system, make more time for fun and enjoyment, learn new skills that are meaningful and challenging, change your current job situation, or just change your perception so you appreciate what you already have. The WDEP system can be used over and over to get what you want in life. This acronym stands for the following:

> ➢ W—exploring your wants, level of commitment, and internal control
> ➢ D—exploring what you doing to get what you want, including thinking, acting, feelings, and attending to your physiology and health
> ➢ E—learning to self-evaluate the linkage to what you want, specific needs to be fulfilled, and effectiveness of overall direction related to identified wants and goals
> ➢ P—continue making plans until eventually successful at achieving goal.

(Wubbolding 2010)

Once you have identified what you want to change, it is helpful to take a look at what increases the likelihood that your thinking and direction of behavior are optimal to actualize your desired want or goal. The following question is vital to set the stage for self-evaluation: "What are you currently doing to get what you want? What specifically have you tried?"

Exploring and evaluating choices and consequences is vital to your success. Ask yourself: "Is what I am doing helping or hurting me?" "Is what I want attainable?" "Am I willing to expend the energy and effort to obtain what I want?" Additional questions that are useful include but are not limited to:

> "Is the overall direction of my life getting me closer or further away from my specific goal?"
> "Are my current choices bringing me closer or further away from the people who are important to me?"
> "Are my current choices helping me or hurting me?"
> "Do my current choices seem reasonable or unreasonable to others?"
> "Are my self-statements effective or ineffective regarding optimal emotional consequences?
> "Does what I want at work align with the organization's vision and strategic plan?"
> "Can I have full control of the choices I want to make?"
> "Are my thoughts and action in harmony with my ethical values?"
> "Is my current level of commitment enough to achieve my goal?"
> "Is there a way I can shrink my goal to daily tasks that I know I can do?"
> "Are my choices helping others as well as myself?"

Making positive changes is easier when your plan is simple, attainable, and measurable, and can be immediately implemented and controlled by you.

Dreams do come true …

Integration Opportunity

How have you made positive changes in the past?

What are the primary ingredients that facilitate growth and development?

What can you do to feel more optimistic about making necessary changes?

Dr. Robert Wubbolding, the director of Reality Therapy, has developed a very helpful process for helping you make the necessary choices in your life that get you closer to pursuing the good life.

Please rank the importance of the following needs:

Love and Belonging—the need for love, intimacy, enjoyable relationships, and support. To care for and feel cared about by friends, family, and close and intimate relationships.

Work/School	Low	1	2	3	4	5	6	7	High
Home/Family	Low	1	2	3	4	5	6	7	High
Friends/Acquaintances	Low	1	2	3	4	5	6	7	High

Self-Worth, Significance, and Recognition—the need for a sense of empowerment, worthiness, and personal effectiveness. To feel able and competent and to be valued and recognized by others.

Work/School	Low	1	2	3	4	5	6	7	High
Home/Family	Low	1	2	3	4	5	6	7	High
Friends/Acquaintances	Low	1	2	3	4	5	6	7	High

Fun and Enjoyment—the need for enjoyment, play, pleasure, and laughter. To do things because they are interesting, absorbing, and stimulating.

Work/School	Low	1	2	3	4	5	6	7	High
Friends/Acquaintances	Low	1	2	3	4	5	6	7	High

Freedom—the need for independence and autonomy to make choices, to create, to explore, and to express oneself freely. To have sufficient space to move around and to feel unrestricted and unrestrained in determination of choices and free will.

Work/School	Low	1	2	3	4	5	6	7	High
Home/Family	Low	1	2	3	4	5	6	7	High
Friends/Acquaintances	Low	1	2	3	4	5	6	7	High

Survival, Health, and Wellness—the need to get your basic needs met and move toward greater states of wellness by making responsible choices regarding physical activity, healthy eating habits, and stress management.

Work/School	Low	1	2	3	4	5	6	7	High
Home/Family	Low	1	2	3	4	5	6	7	High
Friends/Acquaintances	Low	1	2	3	4	5	6	7	High

My wife, Rhonda, and older daughter, Kylee, accomplishing their goal of climbing Harney Peak in the beautiful Black Hills of South Dakota

Quality of Relationships: Loving and Belonging

0 (worst in life).. (best in life) 100

What about the quality of your relationships? Do you appreciate them and want to continue? If you woke up tomorrow with a fantastic social life, what would be different?

Utilization of Gifts and Talents: Feeling Significant

0 (worst in life).. (best in life) 100

What about your current utilization of gifts and talents? Do you appreciate them and want to continue? If you woke up tomorrow going to your dream job, what would it be like?

Seizing the Opportunity to Make Useful Choices: Freedom

0 (worst in life).. (best in life) 100

What are useful choices that you are making and would like to continue? If you woke up tomorrow with an increased commitment to make more responsible choices, what would be different?

Current Level of Energy and Commitment to Wellness: Health and Physiology

0 (worst in life) .... (best in life) 100

What is currently helping you sustain a positive energy that you would like to continue? If you woke up tomorrow with even more positive energy, what would be different?

What is your vision regarding experiencing a quality life in the following areas?

- Love and belonging

- Self-worth, significance, and recognition

- Fun and enjoyment

- Freedom

- Health and Wellness

What do you specifically want in life?

- What do you want that you are not getting?

- What are you getting that you do not want?

- What are the priorities related to what you want?

- What do you have to give up to get what you want?

- How much effort or energy are you willing to exert to get what you want?

- What are you doing that is working or not working for you?

- What are you currently doing to get what you want?

- Tell me about a time when you were getting what you wanted.

- What direction are your choices taking you?

Evaluation of choices:

- Is your overall direction in life the best for you?

- Are your present choices helping or hurting you or others?

- Does it help or hurt you to look at things as you currently do?

- If you could change any behavior, what would it be, and who would be the first to notice?

Developing a plan of action:

- What are your ambivalent feelings about making necessary changes?

- What is possible that you could do?

- What will you do?

Develop a plan that is:

- simple
- attainable
- measurable
- involved
- controlled by the doer of the plan
- committed to

(Wubbolding 2010)

Summary

Knowing the good, loving the good, and doing the good necessitates greater awareness, motivation, and action to promote movement toward feeling good about your life.

The following attitudes and choices have the potential to help increase your wellness and help you pursue the good life:

Live Well:

- Do you have a vision related to pursuing the good life?
- Do you take time to be still and develop a capacity for delight with all that is wonderful in life?
- Can you welcome in the optimal amount of eustress to feel passionate about life?
- Do you have the internal motivation to develop your own wellness program, or do you have a wellness support and accountability system?
- Are you engaged in a workout program that strengthens your entire muscle groups, improves your cardiovascular fitness, and engages appropriate stretching techniques?
- Do you consistently self-evaluate what you want and the ultimate direction your choices are taking you?

Integrity with Relationships:

- Do you give your loved ones time, attention, and affection?

- Do you treat loved ones with admiration and fondness?
- Do you avoid uncontrolled anger, contempt, stonewalling, and power and control?
- Are you a good listener, and can you stay calm when the potential for conflict is high?
- Have you developed rituals with loved ones to reflect on positive relationship memories?
- Do you have an active spiritual or faith life to make your life more meaningful?
- Do you have a plan to stretch your comfort zone and try to bring out the best in others, including yourself?

Finding Meaningful Work:

- Do you fully understand and celebrate your own unique intelligence?
- Have you discovered a career and volunteer activities that utilize your gifts, talents, interests, and other priorities?
- Do you work in an environment that brings out the best in you?
- Have you discovered an optimal balance among work, home, and leisure?
- Are you disciplined regarding your personal finances?

Experiencing a Sense of Purpose:

- Do you believe you are living a life that matters?
- Do you live according to your ethical values?
- Do you treat others the way they want to be treated?
- Do you consistently try to bring out the best in others as well as yourself?
- Are you making the world a better place?
- Do you have a plan for what type of legacy you will leave the world?

It has been said that, "The pain of regret is much greater than the pain of self-discipline." I hope you will take the time to keep hope alive and develop your own *bucket list* of wants and then develop a direction and plan to seize opportunities to make your hopes and dreams come true, with a constant emphasis on reflecting on and enjoying each present moment.

Well, this book is coming to an end, but it is actually just a new beginning for me. It is currently late at night, and I know getting sleep would be good for me; however, I am so excited about this book helping you in some way, whether it be big or small, related to your pursuit of the good life, that I know I can't sleep right now because I have feelings of just feeling happy …

Dr. Mark J. Britzman is a licensed psychologist and clinical mental health counselor. He is a counselor educator at the University of Oklahoma after serving many years as a tenured professor at South Dakota State University. Mark has provided thousands of hours providing professional counseling to individuals, couples, and families; and is a nationally recognized speaker in the areas of promoting psychological health, marital preparation, and character education.

Mark was chosen as an International William Glasser Scholar and received advanced training and certification in Choice Theory/ Reality Therapy to ensure that he can keep his counseling skills at a high level and integrate new research to help others in a pragmatic and meaningful fashion. He also credits the seminal work of Alfred Adler whose ideas and resulting theory was way ahead of its time.

Mark recently received the South Dakota Counseling Association's highest award for service to the counseling profession and the Outstanding Teaching, Advising and Research Award in the College of Education and Human Science at South Dakota State University. The Britzmans were also the recipient of "Fun-Filled Family of the Year" when his children, Kylee and Ali, were young.

Most importantly, however, Mark strives to practice what he preaches and realizes that life is much harder than a typical self-help book would suggest. Although he considers himself a lifelong work in progress, Mark's mission in life is to use his compassionate and encouraging nature to seize opportunities to bring out the best in others.

References

Anchor, Shawn. *The Happiness Advantage.* New York: Crown Publishing Group, 2013.

Ben-Shahar, Tal. *Happier.* New York: McGraw-Hill, 2007.

Brach, Tara. *Radical Acceptance: Embracing Your Life with the Heart of Buddha.* New York: Bantam Books, 2004.

Britzman, Mark, and Wes Hanson. *What Every Educator and Youth Leader Must Know: The Case for Character Education and CHARACTER COUNTS!* Los Angeles: Josephson Institute of Ethics, 2005.

Brooks, David, and Frank Goble. *The Case for Character Education.* Northridge, CA: Studio 4 Productions, 1997.

Carlson, Jon and Michael Maniacci, *Alfred Adler Revisited.* New York: Routledge, 2012.

Carlson, Richard. *Don't Sweat the Small Stuff at Work: Simple Ways to Minimize Stress and Conflict While Bringing Out the Best in Yourself and Others.* New York: Hyperion, 1998.

Covey, Stephen. *Everyday Greatness.* Nashville, TN: Rutledge Hill Press, 2006.

Dweck, Carol. *Mindset: The New Psychology of Success*. New York: Random House, Inc., 2012.

Forsyth, John P., and Georg H. Eifert. *The Mindfulness & Acceptance Workbook for Anxiety*. Oakland, CA: New Harbinger Publications, Inc., 2007.

Fredrickson, Barbara. *Positivity*. New York: Crown Publishers, 2009.

Gardner, Howard. *Frames of Mind: The Theory of Multiple Intelligences*. New York: Basic Books, 2011.

Glasser, William. *Take Charge of Your Life: How to Get What You Want with Choice Theory Psychology*. Bloomington, IN: iUniverse, Inc., 2011.

Goleman, Daniel. *Emotional Intelligence*. New York: Bantam Books, 2006.

Gottman, John. *The Seven Principles for Making Marriage Work: A Practical Guide from the Country's Foremost Relationship Expert*. New York: Three Rivers Press, 2011.

Haidt, Johnathan. *The Happiness Hypothesis*. New York: Basic Books, 2006.

Hanson, Richard. *Hardwiring Happiness*. New York: Harmony, 2013.

Harris, Richard. *The Confidence Gap: A Guide to Overcoming Fear and Self-Doubt*. Boston: Trumpeter Books, 2011.

Henry, Todd. *Die Empty: Unleash Your Best Work Every Day*. New York: Penguin Group, 2013.

Lake, Gina. *From Stress to Stillness: Tools for Inner Peace*. Sedona, AZ: Endless Satsang Foundation, 2013.

Lickona, Thomas, and Matt Davidson. *Smart & Good High Schools: Integrating Excellence and Ethics for Success in School, Work, and Beyond*. Cortland, NY: Center for the 4th and 5th R's. Washington DC: Character Education Partnership, 2005.

Locke, John. *Essay Concerning Human Understanding*. Oxford, UK: Clarendon Press. Book 2, Chapter 21, Section 51. Peter H. Nidditch, ed. of reprinted book. (1689) 1975.

Lyumbomirsky, Sonja. *The How of Happiness: A Scientific Approach to Getting the Life You Want*. New York: The Penguin Press, 2007.

Markman, Howard, Scott Stanley, Susan Blumberg. *Fighting for Your Marriage: A Deluxe Revised Edition of the Classic Best Seller for Enhancing Marriage and Preventing Divorce*. San Francisco: Jossey-Bass, 2010.

Meyers, David G. *The Pursuit of Happiness*. New York: Avon Books, 1992.

Meyers, David G. *The American Paradox: Spiritual Hunger in an Age of Plenty*. New Haven, CT: Yale University Press, 2000.

Miller, William, and Stephen Rollnick. *Motivational Interviewing*. New York: Guildford Press, 2002.

Oettingen, Gabriele. *Rethinking Positive Thinking*. New York: Penguin Group, 2014.

Peterson, Christopher. *Pursuing the Good Life: 100 Reflections on Positive Psychology*. Oxford, NY: Oxford University Press, 2013.

Putnam, Robert. *Bowling Alone: The Collapse and Revival of the American Community*. New York: Simon & Schuster, 2001.

Rath, Tom. *Strengthfinder 2.0*. New York: Gallup Press, 2007.

Rath, Tom. *Eat Move Sleep: Why Small Changes Lead to Big Differences*. Arlington, VA: Missionday, 2013.

Rath, Tom, and Jim Harter. *Well Being: The Five Essential Elements*. New York: Gallup Press, 2010.

Ricard, Matthieu. *Happiness*. New York: Little, Brown and Company, 2011.

Siegel, Dan. *Mindsight: The New Science of Personal Transformation*. New York: Bantam Books, 2011.

Smit, Gary. *Instilling Touchstones of Character*. College Station, TX: Virtualbookworm.com Publishing, Inc., 2014.

Southwick, Steven, and Dennis Charney. *Resilience: The Science of Mastering Life's Greatest Challenges*. Cambridge, NY: Cambridge University Press, 2012.

Schwahn, Chuck, and Bea McGarvey. *Inevitable: Mass Customized Learning*. Charleston: CreateSpace, 2012.

Tileston, Donna. *What Every Teacher Should Know About Student Motivation*. Thousand Oaks, CA: Corwin Press, 2004.

Wehrenberg, Margaret. *The 10 Best-Ever Anxiety Management Techniques*. New York: W.W. Norton & Company, 2008.

Wubbolding, Robert. *Reality Therapy*. Washington DC: American Psychological Association, 2010.

TRUE DIRECTIONS
An affiliate of Tarcher Books

OUR MISSION

Tarcher's mission has always been to publish books
that contain great ideas. Why? Because:

GREAT LIVES BEGIN WITH GREAT IDEAS

At Tarcher, we recognize that many talented authors, speakers,
educators, and thought-leaders share this mission and deserve to be
published – many more than Tarcher can reasonably publish ourselves.
True Directions is ideal for authors and books that increase awareness,
raise consciousness, and inspire others to live their ideals and passions.

Like Tarcher, True Directions books are designed to do three things:
inspire, inform, and motivate.

Thus, True Directions is an ideal way for these important voices to
bring their messages of hope, healing, and help to the world.

Every book published by True Directions– whether it is non-
fiction, memoir, novel, poetry or children's book – continues
Tarcher's mission to publish works that bring positive change
in the world. We invite you to join our mission.

For more information, see the True Directions website:
www.iUniverse.com/TrueDirections/SignUp

Be a part of Tarcher's community to bring positive change in this world!
See exclusive author videos, discover new and exciting books, learn about
upcoming events, connect with author blogs and websites, and more!
www.tarcherbooks.com

TRUE DIRECTIONS
AN AFFILIATE OF TARCHER BOOKS

Printed in the United States
By Bookmasters